MODERN
KOSHER

MODERN KOSHER

Global Flavors, New Traditions

MICHAEL AARON GARDINER

RIZZOLI
NEW YORK

New York · Paris · London · Milan

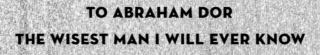

TO ABRAHAM DOR
THE WISEST MAN I WILL EVER KNOW

CONTENTS

INTRODUCTION

Kosher cuisine is about what can be done within a given set of rules. It's a lot more than a specific set of flavors and definitely not just a collection of old recipes sitting on a shelf. Kosher cooks don't spend much time bemoaning the fact that they can't finish a sauce for meat with a pat of butter or the prohibition on pork. There's always something delicious and exciting that *can* be done.

Kosher food is a living, breathing process, not a museum piece. More than that, it's an ongoing process. Kosher cooks apply the laws of *kashrut* to the best available ingredients and flavors, whatever the style and wherever the place. That's how most classic kosher recipes were originally created, and it is how new recipes can be, should be, and are created every day.

That application—part devotional, part practical, always creative and resourceful, always grounded in doing the best you can with what you have—is what kosher cuisine is all about. It's what this book is about.

THE TIDE GOES OUT: THE FUSION NATURE OF DIASPORA FOOD

Another term for this process might be *fusion*. We tend to think of fusion as a chef-driven mash-up, but it is often far more organic than that. Take, for example, the regional American Cajun-Creole or Southwestern cuisines. They resulted from the happy (at least culinarily) collision of peoples together in a new place.

Jews have been cooking fusion for a very long time. As the Jewish people traveled, willingly or otherwise, throughout the world, they carried with them their dietary laws. Forced to adapt the application of those laws to the local ingredients available in these new lands, they engaged in a remarkably fertile exchange of culinary ideas with their hosts. For example, one of Poland's national dishes, *gołąbki* (stuffed cabbage rolls) is likely derived from *holishkes*, a dish prepared by their Jewish neighbors (page 78). Similarly, the very name of the famous Spanish soup gazpacho is likely of Hebrew origin (page 98).

Displaced from their original homes in the process of the diaspora, Jewish families had to find new things to eat in new places all the while observing the laws of kashrut. Ejected from Spain in 1492, they had to go through the same process again. One result was the Eastern European Ashkenazi cuisine so many Americans identify as typical "Jewish cooking" (gefilte fish being but one example; see pages 65 and 68). The Sephardic cuisines of North African and Middle Eastern Jews (with the flavors of tahini and Baharat spices; see pages 159 and 183) are another. But there have been significant Jewish communities throughout the world and in places one might not ever have expected—India, for example, as seen in the Oil-Poached Tuna with Chettinad Curry and Coriander Chutney (page 107).

It is a process that has never stopped and need not do so today.

THE TIDE RETURNS: NEW ISRAELI CUISINE

If that "fusion" process—Jews adapting the laws of kashrut to the geography and cultures of the lands in which they found themselves as the result of one diaspora or another—seemed like the tide going out, then the founding of the State of Israel in 1948 was, at least in part, the tide coming back in. As Jews from throughout the diaspora returned to Israel, they had to do the same process in reverse: take the dishes they had been cooking in Eastern Europe, America, Tunisia, or Yemen and adapt those dishes to the realities of their lives in their new land, Israel. Much of that process, as it had been on the way out, was geography. Some of it was the new neighbors (both Arab and Jewish from different parts of the world). But some of it was spiritual: a return to a place once called home.

The largest group of early immigrants returning home was from the lands of Europe, particularly Eastern Europe. It's thus not surprising that to the limited extent the new state focused on food (as opposed to carving out a country), the flavors of the new country tended to be Ashkenazi. As Yotam Ottolenghi and Michael Solomonov have documented in their books over recent years, as the country has come into its own and as the immigration patterns have changed, Sephardic flavors have come to the fore.

For example, take two dishes that have come to be associated with Israel, shawarma and *shakshuka*. The former is Lebanese in origin and the latter is Tunisian. And yet the Israeli versions of them aren't just the old recipes transplanted to Israel. They are reinterpretations and variations on the originals. The living, ever-changing, fusion nature of Jewish cuisine continues.

THE JEWISH APPROACH TO FOOD

THE LAWS OF KASHRUT

The Jewish dietary laws are the part of *halakha* (Jewish law) governing food. If food is in accordance with the laws of kashrut, it is fit for consumption (the Hebrew word *kashér*, or רָשֵׁב, translates as "fit"). If food violates Jewish law and is unfit for Jews to eat, it is called *treif* (Yiddish, פּיירט, or *treyf*, derived from Hebrew, הַפֶּרָט, or *trēfáh*).

These eight basic rules summarize the laws that govern the Jewish diet and determine what and how Jews can go about eating:

Certain animals may not be eaten at all. For modern cooks, that primarily means no pork and no shellfish.

Permissible birds and mammals must be killed in accordance with Jewish law.

All blood must be drained from meat and poultry or broiled out of it before it is eaten.

Certain parts of permitted animals may not be eaten.

Fruits and vegetables are permitted but must be inspected for bugs (which are not kosher).

Meat (the flesh of birds and mammals) cannot be eaten with dairy (for all practical purposes this means for the entire meal, not just on the same plate). Fish, eggs, fruits, vegetables, and grains can be eaten with either meat or dairy.

Utensils (including pots and pans and other cooking surfaces) that have come into contact with meat may not be used with dairy, and vice versa.

Grape products made by non-Jews may not be eaten. This means that grape products must be kosher certified. Many vendors in large cities specialize in kosher wines and excellent resources, like Online Kosher Wine (onlinekosherwine.com), are making it easier than ever to find them online.

But the laws of kashrut do not just govern which types of foodstuffs Jews can eat; they also address the circumstances of the preparation of the food. That starts at the supermarket. Avoiding treif gets more complex when the home cook does not know how a product was treated between the farm and the store. For example, it may appear to be kosher based on the ingredients, but pots and pans used in preparing it may have been used to cook pork. Widespread kosher certification programs have greatly eased the process: three quarters of all prepackaged foods in the United States and Canada have some kind of kosher certification.

The underlying issue, though, continues on into the home. The same pan cannot blithely be used to cook a cream-based sauce for fish today and an Italian meat sauce for pasta tomorrow. As a practical matter, a kosher home must have two of just about everything. Specifically:

Two sets of dishes and silverware

Two sets of pots and pans

Two sets of tablecloths, placemats, and napkins

There are also issues with how to use the refrigerator, dishwasher, sinks (including materials they can be made from), and more.

While some of these issues can be corrected by specific kashering steps (washing with boiling water, for example), one cannot take a nonkosher kitchen and quickly make it kosher in a practical way. There are steps you can take to prepare a kosher meal on a one-off basis (if, for example, you have observant friends coming for dinner), such as kashering and using aluminum roasting pans and the like, but you wouldn't want to live that way long-term. It is something of an either/or thing. That's not to say people who don't keep a kosher home won't find recipes here to prepare for their kosher friends.

There's an old saying in Jewish society: "Get ten Jews together and you'll have eleven opinions." At least. And the laws of kashrut are no different than any other topic of discussion. The Orthodox disagree with the Conservatives, who disagree with the Reform Jews (and there is a myriad of different opinions within each group) about exactly what it means to keep kosher. The strictest interpretations, of course, hold that absolutely every letter of every law must be followed. Period. Nothing is optional. Others believe that following the details of timing between washing dishwasher loads to keep meat and milk separate is a bit much. Still others observe the laws as to what may be eaten but ignore the necessity of keeping a kosher home. Indeed, at the furthest reach of Reform Judaism the laws of kashrut themselves are optional.

YOU ARE WHAT YOU EAT

Jews have long debated the meaning and reasons for the laws of kashrut. There is no express explanation for them in the Torah. The traditional explanation is that they are among the laws rabbis identified as being without rational explanation (*chukim*) or, put more colloquially, ones God asked Jews to obey as a matter—and act—of devotion. In other words, Jews follow those laws because God commanded them to do so. Others ask whether the kosher laws are health-based. It's easy enough to appreciate rules about the careful separation of meat and dairy in the days before refrigeration. Pork was raised in conditions conducive to salmonella; shellfish and mollusks tend to be bottom and filter feeders which are prone to ingesting contaminated sediments. Each of these would be good explanations for those corresponding prohibitions, and "God said" can be a particularly compelling way of getting a people to engage in or forsake a particular course of conduct.

Perhaps the best explanation is a familiar non-Jewish saying: You are what you eat. At the simplest level, if you keep kosher, you're Jewish. Many—but not all —observant Jews would say it's also true that if you do not keep kosher, you're not Jewish. You are what you eat.

In the eyes of many, the laws of kashrut are identity defining. It's a crucial part of the process—the struggle—of life and, as such, is spiritual in nature. A Jew who keeps kosher cannot simply walk into a supermarket and pull anything he or she wants off the shelf. Rather, he or she must take care at every step along the way.

In that sense, all aspects of eating—even shopping at the supermarket—become part of a surprisingly contemporary and spiritual notion: mindfulness. It's a notion that is implicit in the laws of kosher themselves and finds a particular home in the Kabbalistic tradition. Kabbalah teaches that the soul's nourishment from communing with God is analogous to the body's nourishment from eating. Just as the Kabbalah posits spiritual energy is recycled through the entire system (as demonstrated by the tree of life and the Sephirot), so energy is recycled through the physical act of consuming food. The energy, the life force, of the creature (or plant) we eat adds to our own energy, our own life force.

The contemplative, purposeful eating the Kabbalists describe is, ultimately, a matter of mindfulness. Indeed, as the Kabbalists see it, at least at one level, the "fitness" involved in kashrut might best be described as spiritual fitness—being one with God. This spiritual approach to food is at the heart of kosher cuisine and possibly the best explanation for the laws of kashrut. You are what you eat. What you eat can be absolutely anything that is permissible within the laws of kashrut.

HOW TO USE THIS BOOK

It is likely that few people will open this book to page one and work their way through the book slavishly cooking each and every recipe. That tends not to be how home cooks work in today's world. Today's home cook is more likely to head directly to a cookbook's index (or photographs) than to the first recipe or even the table of contents. He or she will look for a particular ingredient—say, chicken—in search of an idea for their next evening meal. Who isn't looking for something new to do with chicken? This book offers several ideas, including Pho Ga with Matzo Noodles (page 30), Roast Chicken with Schmaltz Massage and Le Puy Lentils (page 73), and Smoked Chicken Hush Puppies with Remoulade and Gremolata (page 104).

The cook may not end up making any of those dishes for dinner, but each of the recipes includes at least one idea they could incorporate into that dinner. From the use of Vietnamese spices in the *pho ga* (a.k.a. chicken pho), which could easily form the basis for a sauce to the use of schmaltz as a straight-up butter substitute in the roast chicken to the idea of stuffing a hush puppy with chicken (smoked or unsmoked). That's without getting into the gremolata—an easy flavor booster that can accompany many different main courses—or something that could totally change the next Seder, like matzo noodles.

My goal is inspiration as much as replication. It's my genuine hope that for nearly every center-of-the-plate, star ingredient this book will offer interesting and delicious flavor combinations and new-to-you techniques and approaches (or all of them) to bring to your dinner table. That is, after all, pretty much exactly how Jewish cuisine has evolved over the years.

One thing you will not find in this book, however, is desserts. It's just not the way I eat. I'm not sugar-phobic; sugar is just not where I choose to spend my calories. When my family finishes a meal with something sweet, it tends to be some berries (with or without a dollop of fresh cream), stone fruit (with or without a drizzle of good balsamic vinegar), or fresh mango (with or without a sprinkling of Tajin).

While I myself may not boast a sweet tooth, there is a grand tradition of Jewish confections and desserts. From *sufganiyot* (jam-filled Hanukkah doughnuts without those annoying holes in the middle) to chocolate babka (the result of what happens when bread and chocolate acknowledge each other as soulmates) to the grand Jewish cookie tradition (with coconut macaroons and rugelach leading the charge) and *ashuplados* (Sephardic meringue clouds).

If you're looking for ways to turn nonkosher desserts kosher, ingredient substitution is a good strategy. The central problem in kosher desserts isn't that the dishes themselves are not kosher—there aren't many pork or shellfish desserts, nor ones combining meat and milk—as much as it is what dishes the dessert follows and whether that allows you to use dairy elements. If it does, there are few problems. If it doesn't, there are a number of very well-established ways of taking non-Jewish desserts and kosher-izing them. For example, replacing butter with coconut oil and cream with coconut cream. Aside from a number of good books on kosher cuisine that include excellent dessert chapters, another great resource is vegan cookbooks.

Also, on the topic of how I eat (or choose not to eat): I don't keep a kosher kitchen. In fact, I don't keep kosher. I am a Reform Jew and have been my whole life (except for a few years as a teen at a Conservative synagogue). For me, Judaism has been a function of (1) the fact I'm the son of a family that was very directly affected by the Holocaust and (2) food. Learning what is possible and beautiful and delicious within the laws of kashrut has been my deepest form of Jewish study. But in studying those laws I view them less as some sort of restriction or limitation than as a spur to creativity.

The key to using the Jewish dietary laws to kickstart creativity is exploration. That is what this book is about: exploring what is possible within kashrut. The recipes here are ideas and spurs to the formation of other ideas. There's no reason you couldn't use short ribs from the goulash (page 87) instead of lamb shanks for the *birria* (page 85). Just adjust the cooking time accordingly. Perhaps you bought some really good fish but feel like that ultimate comfort food, pozole. Take the recipe for Duck Pozole Rojo (page 129) and swap in your fish.

One of my favorite discoveries in my forays into vegan cookery is nutritional yeast, deactivated *Saccharomyces cerevisiae*. It provides a cheesy, nutty flavor to any dish and does so without having to use a dairy product. That alone makes it a huge asset in the kosher kitchen. You can sprinkle it as a finishing element (try it with popcorn and you'll likely be addicted), use it anywhere you'd use cheese, or add it to just about any preparation for a bit of extra depth of flavor.

In several of the recipes in this book—including Involtini of Eggplant and Pine Nut "Ricotta" (page 56) and Baharat Roasted Cauliflower with Pickled Red Cabbage and Pumpkin Seed Sauce (page 63)—I show different ways to adapt nut cheese techniques I've borrowed from the world of vegan cuisine. There are many more things you could do riffing on those ideas. Add a little more nutritional yeast to either of those recipes and spread it on top of a hamburger, for example, and you have a . . . nutcheeseburger. Or take the pelmeni from page 49 and use a filling of pine nut "ricotta" and potato instead.

There are a handful of ingredients that I find really help amp up the flavor profile of many dishes (kosher or otherwise)—J. Kenji López-Alt of Serious Eats calls ingredients like these "flavor bombs." One of these is fish sauce. A drop or two of fish sauce adds an amazing, ineffable depth to a sauce or soup because of its umami (the fifth of the five basic flavors, after sweet, salty, sour, and bitter, often described as the essence of savory). Just as you wouldn't chow down on a can of anchovies in oil but would happily rinse, chop, and use some in a sauce or dressing, fish sauce is the best supporting actor or actress, not the star of the show. It makes everything around it better. As of this writing there is only one brand of fish sauce that is certified kosher that I am aware of. Fortunately, it is one of the best: Red Boat.

But don't stop with fish sauce. Take it to the next level and use that fish sauce to make the recipe for *garum* on page 169. The inclusion of various spices (which you can and should feel free to alter and play with to your taste) adds still another level to that which fish sauce can accomplish on its own.

Other umami-rich ingredients can provide similar hits of flavor and depth; some subtle, others less so. Try adding a small amount of Marmite or soy sauce to a pasta sauce, for example. Miso intensifies the salty-savory-sweet depth of flavor of any sauce or dressing. Each of these is an ingredient that just makes everything it's used in taste better.

Also, at the back of the book are a number of pantry ingredients. While some of these are only used in one or two recipes in this book, the fact is, they are, to some extent, mix-and-match candidates. You could use Sofregit (page 167) as a sauce with any rice or other grain dish or in place of mirepoix in any soup or almost any sauce. Several other of the sauces in that section are in the nature of "hot sauces." Feel free to swap one out for another and make your own new creation.

As you go through the recipes in this book, there are a few important assumptions and ideas that are implicit in all the recipes:

- **ALL MEATS MUST BE KOSHER** (indeed, all ingredients must be). So, for example, if the recipe says "chicken," it must be read to mean "kosher chicken." That means finding a kosher butcher. Many larger cities have kosher butcher shops. Even grocery chains in some of those cities will have certain stores with kosher meat sections (or, if not, they might at least carry kosher chicken). If you don't live near any of those, ordering online from sources like Glatt Kosher Store (glattkosherstore.com), Grow & Behold (growandbehold.com), or KOL Foods (kolfoods.com) may be your best bet.

- **FOR DISHES THAT INCLUDE INGREDIENTS LIKE CHICKEN LIVER,** those ingredients must be properly kashered. That means they must be properly roasted to eliminate all the blood in accordance with Jewish law.

- **ALL PREPARED PRODUCTS MUST BE KOSHER.** Just because an ingredient in its raw and fresh form (say a fruit or vegetable) would be kosher does not necessarily mean that a prepared product featuring that ingredient is kosher. Fortunately, as most observant Jews are aware, there are a number of agencies that certify products that are prepared in accordance with the laws of kashrut and allow those products to advertise the fact that they're kosher by using that agency's "bug" (logo) on their label. Look for those.

- **ALL SALT USED IN THIS BOOK'S RECIPES,** unless clearly specified otherwise, is Diamond Crystal brand kosher salt. While Morton kosher salt is an excellent product, it cannot be swapped in for Diamond Crystal kosher salt at a 1:1 ratio by volume (but they *can* be swapped interchangeably by weight). Morton salt crystals are larger, so the same volume of Morton will taste substantially saltier—almost twice as salty—than Diamond Crystal. Of course, different people have different palates. At the end of the day, season for salinity to your palate and your preference. While there are a few recipes that I specifically intend you to salt heavily—New York Strip Steak with Mushroom and Red Wine Reduction (page 143), for example—it is generally wise to season conservatively at every step along the way and adjust the seasoning at the end of a recipe.

- **AND SALT IS NOT THE ONLY "SEASONING"** in a dish that needs to be adjusted (perhaps more accurately, balanced). Acid should, too. Just as it "pulls" flavor from the ingredients in a dish, acid (think vinegar or citrus) cuts through fat and balances salty and sweet flavors. The final step in every single dish in this book (for that matter, every dish you ever make) should be to balance the flavors. To do that, adjust both the salt and acid.

- **ALL BUTTER IS UNSALTED.**

- **MY PORTIONS TEND TO BE ON THE SMALLER SIDE** because I like offering more dishes per meal with smaller amounts of food per dish. If you want to go with a standard appetizer-main-dessert program, do it and serve larger portions along the way.

Similarly, there are a few notes on particular equipment to consider:

- **FIRST,** throughout this book I often call for the use of a high-speed blender or food processor. For puréed soups or sauces, I tend to use a Vitamix. My basic reasons for this preference are the sheer power of its motor and the superior, refined texture of the purée the variable-speed control produces. You, however, can use whatever you like: an immersion blender, a food processor, a drink blender, or Ninja. Passing the product of one of these through a fine-mesh strainer, although an extra step, can yield an equally good if not superior final product (albeit with additional effort).

- **SECOND,** while I live in San Diego, where the weather allows "grilling season" all year, that is clearly not the case everywhere. So, where I call for smoking ingredients (for example, the Smoked Chicken Hush Puppies on page 109), I suggest a smoking gun—a remarkably convenient gadget that quickly and efficiently infuses relatively small amounts of product with the smoky flavors of your choice, even in the dead of winter. I use the PolyScience Hand-Held Smoke Infuser.

- **THIRD,** while I love the flavor and poetry of grilling and the technical perfection of the reverse-sear method of meat cookery, my go-to for cooking steaks is sous vide. Adapted from industrial processes, the food (here, the steaks) is sealed in food-grade plastic bags and cooked slowly in water to a specific internal temperature. The primary advantage is that the entire piece of meat from its surface to its center is cooked to the exact same degree. It's all "the good part." A quick, high-temperature sear to caramelize the outside gives the perfect finish. There are a number of brands of very good home sous vide machines. Mine is made by Anova (and I highly recommend it), but Joule is also good as well.

This book is mine as I write these words. Once you buy it, though, it's yours. It has never been my intention to write a comprehensive bible of kosher food or guide to a kosher lifestyle. It's been my goal to help people see kosher cooking as a world of possibilities rather than a set of limitations. Go play in the kitchen!

JEWISH AND ISRAELI RECIPES

FOR THE MODERN TABLE

SMALL
PLATES

sraelis tend to call it "Arab salad," even though the rest of the world calls it "Israeli salad." I call it delicious. But I couldn't help but think the acid from the tomatoes made the classic vinaigrette dressing surplus to requirements. Instead, I chose to pair it with the creaminess of a fresh herb ranch dressing (slightly less sweet than a traditional ranch), which addresses that point.

ISRAELI SALAD WITH FRESH HERB RANCH DRESSING

SERVES 4 TO 6

25 to 30 cherry tomatoes, quartered (about 2 cups)

Salt

2 Persian cucumbers (or 1 English cucumber), diced (about 2 cups)

¼ cup finely chopped shallots

¼ to ½ cup Fresh Herb Ranch Dressing (page 174)

Vinegar or fresh lemon juice (optional)

Place the tomatoes on a plate, cut side up, and salt them. Place the cucumbers on another plate, cut side up, and salt them, too. Let the tomatoes and cucumbers sit until they release their liquid, at least 30 minutes.

Rinse the salt and any clinging liquid from the tomatoes and cucumbers. In a large bowl, combine the tomatoes, cucumbers, and chopped shallots. Add ¼ cup of the dressing and toss gently to coat. Taste the salad and adjust the seasonings accordingly by adding salt, more dressing, or a splash of vinegar or squeeze of lemon.

This dish is named for my great-uncle Abraham Dor, one of Israel's first state engineers and the wisest man I ever knew. It's a version of a dish I've enjoyed since childhood, and it's one I imagine Abe's mother making: a comfort food for him as it is for me. One advantage of a family heirloom dish like this—one passed down from generation to generation and transplanted across three continents (from Egypt to Europe to the United States)—is that there's no pressure to make it just the way Grandma made it. Because there is no definitive version, there's no reason not to innovate. I have no doubt the version I make today is different from the one Abe ate as a child.

The essence of the dish is the textural contrasts between the chickpeas and hard-boiled eggs (which soften and fall apart to enrich the dressing). For this version I added spinach in order to riff on the classic Middle Eastern combination of chickpeas and spinach. The use of Belgian endive as a serving vessel—boats in which to serve the salad—lends an air of elegance to this humble salad.

ABE'S EGGS: CHICKPEA, HARD-BOILED EGG, AND SPINACH SALAD IN BELGIAN ENDIVE

SERVES 4

FOR THE SALAD:

2 cups spinach leaves

3 hard-boiled eggs

1 (15-ounce) can chickpeas

½ teaspoon fresh thyme leaves

1 teaspoon fresh oregano leaves

FOR THE DRESSING:

Juice of 1 medium lemon (plus more as needed)

¼ cup extra-virgin olive oil

Salt and freshly ground pepper

1 teaspoon Spanish sweet paprika (or more to taste)

FOR PLATING:

8 attractive Belgian endive leaves, bases trimmed

TO MAKE THE SALAD: Bring a pot of water to a boil over high heat and prepare an ice bath in a large bowl. Wash and de-stem the spinach. Blanch the spinach in boiling water for just long enough for the spinach to lose its texture, about 30 seconds. Remove the spinach from the water, immediately shock in the ice bath, then drain well, dry the spinach, and chop it.

Shell and dice the hard-boiled eggs and set aside. Rinse the chickpeas and set them aside as well.

TO MAKE THE DRESSING: In a small bowl, whisk together the lemon juice and olive oil and season with salt and pepper and the paprika. Taste the dressing and adjust with salt and/or more lemon juice as needed.

TO SERVE: In a large bowl, combine the chopped spinach, eggs, chickpeas, and herbs. Drizzle with the dressing and lightly toss to coat. Spoon the salad into the Belgian endive "boats" for serving.

ather than the familiar Ukrainian beet version, my wife's family's Polish borscht is made with *Boletus* mushrooms (think porcinis), which gives it a deep umami-rich character. Clarifying the soup into a consommé, a classic French technique that's actually quite easy, elevates the hearty peasant dish into an elegant starter. Dried beet strips add both a beautiful color and hint of earthy sweetness, and the chervil garnish adds a delicate anise-like note. Really, though, the hardest part of this recipe is keeping in mind to start it a day ahead.

MUSHROOM BORSCHT CONSOMMÉ WITH DRIED BEET STRIPS AND CHERVIL

SERVES 4

FOR THE DRIED BEET STRIPS:

2 large beets

Salt

FOR THE MUSHROOM CONSOMMÉ:

2 ounces dried porcini mushrooms

1 large onion, diced

2 leeks, white parts only, cleaned, quartered lengthwise, and thinly sliced

2 medium carrots, diced

2 ribs celery, diced

1 bulb fennel, cored and diced (fronds and stalks reserved for another purpose)

1 tablespoon extra-virgin olive oil

Salt

1 bay leaf

3 medium tomatoes, cored and chopped

1 pound button mushrooms, sliced

4 large egg whites

Fresh chervil leaves (or parsley or fennel fronds) for garnish

TO MAKE THE DRIED BEET STRIPS: At least one day before serving the dish, preheat the oven to 200°F or its lowest setting and line a baking sheet with parchment paper. (Alternatively, you can use a countertop food dehydrator set at 140°F; follow the machine instructions.)

Peel and thinly slice the beets into rounds about ⅛ inch thick. Slice the rounds into strips about 1 inch long. Transfer to the prepared baking sheet (or dehydrator tray) and bake for at least 6 hours (and up to overnight if using a dehydrator), until the beets are firm but neither rubbery nor crispy. Season the beet strips with salt and set aside. The dried beet strips can be kept in an airtight container at room temperature overnight or in the refrigerator for up to 1 week. They make a wonderful snack; so much so, in fact, that I really don't know how long they can last. I'm not sure they ever made it to the one-week mark without being eaten.

TO MAKE THE MUSHROOM CONSOMMÉ: In a small bowl, cover the porcini mushrooms with 1 cup boiling water and let stand for 15 minutes to rehydrate. Remove the mushrooms with a fork and pat dry, discarding the liquid. Combine the onion, leeks, carrots, celery, and fennel with the olive oil in a large soup pot or Dutch oven, season with salt (start with about 1 teaspoon) and sweat the vegetables over low heat until softened but not browned, about 5 minutes. Add the bay leaf and tomatoes and cook for another 5 minutes, or until the tomatoes lose their texture. Add the button mushrooms and 8 cups water and bring to a boil over high heat. Reduce the heat and simmer until it takes on a deep flavor that just shouts MUSHROOM, at least 1 hour, but as much as 3 hours, depending on your desired intensity and the quality of the mushrooms.

(continued)

Pour the stock through a conical or fine-mesh strainer into a large bowl, pressing on the solids to extract as much liquid as possible. Discard the solids. Let the stock cool, then cover and transfer to the refrigerator and chill until it is fully cooled, at least 1 hour or up to 4 hours.

Transfer the chilled stock to a medium pot. Place the egg whites in a medium bowl and whip until just starting to foam. Whisk the beaten egg whites into the stock and set over medium heat. Bring the stock just to a gentle simmer, stirring occasionally. Don't let it reach a full boil. A "raft" will appear on the surface as the proteins in the egg whites coagulate—you'll know it when you see it. This raft is the engine that cleanses the broth by gathering the impurities. As this happens, stop stirring and let the stock simmer gently for about 30 minutes, adjusting the heat to keep it below a full boil.

Carefully agitate the bottom of the pot with a spatula to loosen any raft that may be caught. Simmer the broth gently for about 5 minutes, breaking the surface of the raft as necessary to allow some of the pressure to escape. When the raft is solid and you can no longer see impurities rising to the surface, remove the pan from the heat. Using a ladle, pass the clear liquid off through a fine-mesh strainer into another soup pot. Taste for seasoning and adjust accordingly.

TO SERVE: Gather dried beet strips into a small mound in the center of each bowl, topping each with chervil leaves. Gently ladle the consommé into the bowls until it comes about two-thirds of the way up the nest. The beet strips will begin to soften in the hot liquid, releasing a cloud of red color into the consommé. Serve immediately—ladle the consommé into each bowl at the table, for extra drama, so each guest can see the bloom.

t's an annual Passover matzo-ball conundrum: "sinkers" or "floaters" for matzo balls. Both are valid choices, at least in theory, but if I wanted a heavy ball in my soup, I'd go with Mexican *albondigas* (meatballs).

I knew the theory of floaters, at least part of which involves incorporating beaten egg whites (along with seltzer water and baking powder) into the matzo balls to make them light, fluffy, and airy. The issues were not beating the egg whites enough or incorporating the solids into the egg whites too heavily. So, I knew I would have to beat the egg whites nearly to the point of stiff peaks. I would also have to be very, very gentle in folding in the matzo meal.

But I also had a trick up my sleeve, a little bit of modernist cuisine. Not the whizbang, smoke and mirrors showmanship side of it but, rather, the practical side. The substance in egg whites that lets them do their magic is called lecithin. It is an excellent emulsifier. One of the basic tools of the modern gastronomy arsenal is soy lecithin, which is available at vitamin and supplement stores like GNC or online from such exotic retailers as Walmart (and which is kosher for Passover according to Sephardic Jews but not most Ashkenazis). So, to amp up the effect of the egg whites, I decided to kick up my matzo balls with a tablespoon of soy lecithin. The result was floating, pillowy matzo balls.

TOMATO MATZO BALL SOUP WITH PICKLED GARLIC CHIVES

SERVES 4 TO 6

FOR THE PICKLED GARLIC CHIVES:

4 to 6 garlic chives

1 teaspoon salt

1 teaspoon brown sugar

¼ cup apple cider vinegar

FOR THE SOUP:

6 medium tomatoes

2 large white onions, quartered

3 cloves garlic, peeled

3 tablespoons grapeseed, canola, or another neutral oil

2 leeks, white parts only, cleaned, quartered lengthwise, and thinly sliced

8 cups Chicken Stock (page 151)

2 jalapeño chiles, seeded and sliced

Juice of 4 key limes

TO MAKE THE PICKLED GARLIC CHIVES: Trim the garlic chives to about 3 inches, or wherever the chive stems get excessively fibrous. Combine the salt, brown sugar, and vinegar in a large bowl and whisk to fully dissolve the solids.

Bring a saucepan of water to boil over high heat. Add the garlic chives to the boiling water and blanch until their color brightens, about 15 seconds. Do not let them fully wilt. Immediately transfer the garlic chives to the pickling liquid, adding water as needed to cover. Refrigerate for 30 minutes.

TO MAKE THE SOUP: Preheat the oven to 350°F and line a baking sheet with parchment paper.

Place the tomatoes, onions, and garlic on the prepared sheet and roast until blistered and the onions begin to brown, about 30 minutes.

(continued)

FOR THE MATZO BALLS:

3 large eggs

1 tablespoon grapeseed, canola, or another neutral oil

1 tablespoon seltzer water

½ cup matzo meal

1 teaspoon salt

1 tablespoon soy lecithin

½ teaspoon baking powder

In a large soup pot, sweat the leeks in the oil over low heat until just translucent, about 3 minutes. Add the roasted vegetables and chicken stock and bring to a boil over high heat. Reduce to a simmer and cook for 15 minutes.

TO MAKE THE MATZO BALLS: While the soup is cooking, separate the egg whites from the yolks, reserving the yolks, and transfer the whites to the bowl of a stand mixer fitted with the whisk attachment. Beat the whites on high speed until they form stiff peaks, about 5 minutes. Whisk the oil and seltzer into the reserved yolks and gently fold into the whites. Combine the matzo meal, salt, soy lecithin, and baking powder in a medium bowl and fold into the egg mixture as gently as possible using a plastic spatula. Refrigerate for 30 minutes.

Meanwhile, line another baking sheet with parchment paper. Remove the matzo ball material from the refrigerator. Working with moist hands (have a bowl of water handy to refresh), take a heaping tablespoon of the matzo ball material and form into a ball. Repeat with the remaining matzo ball material.

TO FINISH THE SOUP AND SERVE: Bring the soup back to a boil and gently add the matzo balls to the pot. Reduce the heat, add the chiles and lime juice, and simmer, uncovered, for 10 minutes. Ladle the soup into soup bowls. Float 2 or 3 matzo balls in each bowl and garnish with the garlic chives.

NOTE: Many Ashkenazi Jews will look at this recipe and ask (at the very least) whether soy lecithin—made, of course, from soybeans—is kosher for Passover. Spoiler alert: It depends. Ashkenazi rabbis have long treated beans as among the foods that are otherwise kosher but because they involve (or might appear to involve) leavening are not kosher for Passover, or *chametz*. Ashkenazi Jews also see rice, corn, legumes, and some other foodstuffs that rise in response to contact with water (*kitniyot*) as chametz. Sephardic Jews, on the other hand, do consume kitniyot on Passover.

In the past, in the United States, this was not a significant issue. Once again, though, Israel comes into play. While the majority of American (indeed world) Jews are Ashkenazi, the majority of Israeli Jews are Sephardic. That has had a significant effect on the worldwide Jewish perception of such issues.

t is not for nothing chicken noodle soup is called "Jewish penicillin." It is, perhaps, the prototypical Jewish food. Whether there is actually something medicinal about the stuff or it's the placebo effect (a.k.a. the comfort food factor) is quite beside the point. It works because it's wonderful.

But I don't get to have the old Jewish penicillin very often. On the other hand, the next month that goes by without my having a bowl or three of *pho*—the magical Vietnamese noodle soup—will be a first in recent memory. While I'm particularly passionate about the classic beef versions, there's real beauty in the chicken version (*pho ga*) as well. Where beef pho speaks of the muscular, chicken pho whispers of delicacy. When made with craft and care, pho ga achieves that delicacy but does so with a broth that still manages to taste like the liquified essence of chicken. It is soothing and taps deep into the comfort vein.

But pho ga with matzo balls would just be matzo ball soup with Vietnamese spices. Not that there's anything wrong with that. To make it more than that, though, it takes noodles: matzo meal and rice flour noodles. This is, no doubt, a laborious, time-consuming recipe. Pho is. Homemade pasta is. That's just the way it is. But with those noodles, it becomes possible to see just how very good the mash-up of pho and Jewish penicillin can be. And if you're not up for it, just use the matzo balls from the previous recipe.

PHO GA WITH MATZO NOODLES (VIETNAMESE "JEWISH PENICILLIN")

SERVES 4 TO 6

FOR THE BROTH:

1 whole onion, unpeeled

2-inch chunk ginger, unpeeled

1 whole chicken (4 to 5 pounds)

2 tablespoons coriander seeds

4 whole cloves

2 pieces star anise

2 tablespoons brown sugar

2 tablespoons fish sauce

Stems from 1 small bunch cilantro, tied into a bunch with twine

FOR THE MATZO NOODLES:

1 cup matzo meal

2 tablespoons rice flour

2 large eggs plus 1 large yolk

3 tablespoons water

2 tablespoons extra-virgin olive oil

Potato starch for dusting

TO MAKE THE BROTH: Holding them with tongs or suspending them over a gas burner on the stovetop set to medium heat (and your fan going), roast the ginger and onion until blackened on all sides. (Alternatively, preheat the oven to 400°F and line a baking sheet with aluminum foil. Arrange the top rack so that the top of the onion will be about 4 inches from the top burning element. Cut the onion in half, but do not peel it, and put it on the prepared baking sheet. Transfer to the oven and roast until the onion skin chars and the ginger softens, about 30 minutes. Remove from the oven and let cool.) Once cooled, remove the blackened skin from the onion and, using a spoon or the back of a butter knife, peel the ginger, then slice it into thick coins.

As the ginger and onion are roasting, fill a large stockpot with water and bring to a boil over high heat. Using a sharp knife, remove the breast meat from the chicken. Refrigerate the chicken breast. With a cleaver or heavy chef's knife, chop the rest of the chicken, including the legs, wings, and back, into 3-inch sections (you can also ask the butcher to do this for you). When the water boils, add the chopped chicken pieces (holding back the breast meat) and boil just until the foam rises to the surface, about 5 minutes. This is normal, expected, and desired to achieve a clearer broth. Drain the pot, discarding the

FOR THE SOUP BOWL:

½ cup thinly sliced white onion, soaked in ice water for 30 minutes

Thinly sliced scallions (green parts only)

FOR THE ACCOMPANIMENTS:

2 cups bean sprouts (or pea shoots), rinsed

Fresh cilantro leaves

Fresh basil (or, preferably Thai basil) leaves

1 lime, cut into wedges

Sriracha sauce

Hoisin sauce

Pickled Serrano Chiles (page 179)

liquid. Wash the pot to make sure that none of the foam remains. Once cool, rinse the chicken free of any foam.

In a clean soup pot or Dutch oven, combine 2 quarts water, the chopped chicken pieces, reserved breast meat, onion, ginger, coriander, cloves, star anise, brown sugar, fish sauce, and cilantro stems. Bring just to a boil over medium-high heat, then immediately reduce the heat to low and partially cover.

Simmer for about 15 minutes, then check the chicken breasts to see if the white meat has fully cooked; once cooked, remove the breasts and let cool. Once cooled enough to handle, shred the breast meat into bite-sized pieces and refrigerate the meat for later in the recipe. Continue simmering the broth for 3 to 4 hours, until it reduces to one-third the original volume. As the broth reduces, skim any foam off the top with a slotted spoon approximately every 20 minutes—a clear broth is a sign of good pho. Taste and adjust the seasoning with more fish sauce or brown sugar.

TO MAKE THE MATZO NOODLES: While the broth simmers, combine the matzo meal, rice flour, eggs, yolk, water and olive oil in the bowl of a stand mixer fitted with the dough hook attachment and mix on low speed to combine. Turn to speed 2 and knead until a dough forms, about 4 minutes. Cover dough with a dish towel and let it rest for 20 to 30 minutes.

Using either a manual pasta roller or a pasta sheet roller attachment to your stand mixer, set it to #1 and run the pasta dough through the roller. While on #1, fold the dough in half and run it through again (better yet, repeat this step several times). Dust the dough with potato starch on each side. Change the roller's setting to #2 and pass the dough through. Do this twice, and then twice each on #3 and then #4.

Once again, dust your pasta sheet with potato starch. Cut your pasta either using a knife or a dough cutting attachment to your stand mixer. To do so by hand with a knife, roll the pasta sheet into a tube and flatten it. With a sharp knife, cut across the flattened tube to form ¼-inch pasta strips (tagliatelle). There's no reason you couldn't choose a wider pasta shape.

TO FINISH THE SOUP AND SERVE: Strain the pho broth through a fine-mesh sieve into another clean soup pot. Discard the solids. Bring the broth back to a boil over medium heat and return the shredded chicken breast meat back into the broth. Bring a medium pot of water to a boil and cook the noodles to al dente, 3 to 4 minutes.

To serve, divide the noodles among bowls and top with sliced white onions, scallions, and pho broth. Serve with the accompaniments alongside.

Chopped chicken liver is another Ashkenazi classic. This preparation elevates the original a bit by balancing the richness of the livers with the acidity of the pickled onions and radish sprouts, adding a touch of heat and textural interest. It's chopped chicken liver more the way you might get it at a San Sebastian tapas bar, where *montaditos* ("bites on bread") are an entire class of *pintxos* (the Basque word for tapas).

CHOPPED CHICKEN LIVER MONTADITO WITH PICKLED ONIONS AND RADISH SPROUTS

MAKES ABOUT 1½ QUARTS

FOR THE CHOPPED CHICKEN LIVER:

10 tablespoons Schmaltz (page 187) (plus extra for drizzling on the baguette slices)

1 onion, finely chopped

2 pounds chicken livers, trimmed

Salt and freshly ground black pepper

¼ cup dry white wine (such as sauvignon blanc or a white rioja)

2 large hard-boiled eggs, peeled and coarsely chopped

2 tablespoons finely chopped fresh parsley

FOR PLATING:

1 French baguette

Pink Pickled Onions (page 177)

Radish sprouts (or microgreens), for garnish

Preheat oven to 375°F.

Melt 6 tablespoons of the schmaltz in a large sauté pan over medium-low heat. Add the onion and cook, stirring occasionally, until softened and just starting to brown, about 10 minutes. Season the livers with salt and pepper, then raise the heat to high and add the livers to the pan with the onion. Cook, turning occasionally, until the livers are just pink inside (check one with a paring knife), about 8 minutes. Add the wine to the pan and cook off the wine.

Transfer the contents of the pan to the bowl of a food processor. Let the livers cool slightly, add the chopped hard-boiled eggs, and pulse until the livers are finely chopped but not completely puréed. Add the parsley and the remaining 4 tablespoons of schmaltz and pulse to combine. Season with salt and pepper.

Transfer the chopped liver to a bowl. Press plastic wrap onto the surface so that air has no access and refrigerate until chilled.

Meanwhile, line a baking sheet with parchment paper. Slice the baguette ½ inch thick on the diagonal. Arrange the slices in a single layer on the baking sheet and brush the tops with the additional schmaltz. Toast the slices until golden and crisp, 8 to 10 minutes. Remove from the oven and let cool.

Top each baguette slice with a generous spoonful of chopped liver swiped across it. Garnish with pickled onions and radish sprouts, arrange on a platter, and serve.

This dish is the mash-up of two prototypical Jewish elements and two that definitely don't seem to be likely suspects. But the acidity and sweetness of the pickled blackberries combine with the piquant quality of the wasabi and rich sweetness of the cream to perfectly complement the latkes and smoked salmon.

While the latkes may be a classical Jewish ingredient, the technique I use here is anything but. Instead of grating all the ingredients and then frying them together, I use a more typical hash brown technique and parboil the potatoes before grating them. Then I put them (mixed with the onion) in a ring mold and lightly press them using the bottom of a wine glass. This technique allows for greater precision and a more even cook. It also helps prevent an experience most Jews have had at least once at a Hanukkah supper: thin, gorgeous, delicious-looking latkes that fall apart as mom tries to serve you from the platter. Even if you don't use the rest of the recipe, definitely try that technique.

LATKES WITH SMOKED SALMON, PICKLED BLACKBERRY, AND WASABI CREAM

SERVES 6 (MAKES 18 LATKES)

FOR THE WASABI CREAM:

¼ cup sour cream

1 teaspoon wasabi paste

1 teaspoon apple cider vinegar

FOR THE LATKES:

2 medium waxy potatoes (1½ to 1¾ pounds), unpeeled

1 medium onion, finely grated

4 large eggs

1 tablespoon potato starch

1 teaspoon baking powder

1 teaspoon kosher salt

1 teaspoon freshly ground black pepper

Grapeseed, canola, or another neutral oil, for frying

¾ pound smoked salmon lox (or, better yet, homemade gravlax), cut into 1½ by ½-inch pieces

Pickled Blackberries (page 180)

TO MAKE THE WASABI CREAM: In a small bowl, whisk together the sour cream, wasabi paste, and vinegar until combined. This can be made up to a day ahead, covered, and refrigerated until ready to use.

TO MAKE THE LATKES: Place the potatoes in a large saucepan, add cold water to cover, and bring to a boil over high heat. Ready an ice bath while the water boils. Cook the potatoes until they are just tender and can be easily pierced with a sharp knife, 15 to 20 minutes. Drain and immediately transfer the potatoes to the ice bath for at least 5 minutes. Once cooled, drain and dry the potatoes (do not peel) and transfer to the refrigerator, uncovered (so the potatoes dry), for at least 1 hour and up to overnight.

Using a food processor fitted with the shredding disk or the large holes on a box grater, shred the potatoes and transfer to a large bowl. Add the grated onion, eggs, potato starch, baking powder, salt, and pepper and mix to combine.

Heat 1 tablespoon oil in a large nonstick skillet over medium-high heat until just shimmering. Pat 2 to 3 tablespoons (depending on the size latke you want) of the latke mixture into a small disk and

(continued)

fry in the hot oil, about 2 minutes per side, to test for seasoning and adjust accordingly. Form the remaining mixture into latkes just as you did the tester. It is best to form the latkes just before you cook them. If you want less rustic and more precisely shaped latkes, scoop the mixture into a 3-inch ring mold (or a clean and empty tuna can with the bottom cut out), then use the bottom of a white wine glass to lightly pat it down. Place the formed latkes on a parchment-lined baking sheet as you make them.

To fry the latkes, heat the skillet over medium-high heat until hot, then add two tablespoons oil to the hot skillet and swirl to coat the entire pan. Working quickly, add up to four latkes per batch to the pan and cook until they are nicely browned, about 2 to 3 minutes per side. If using the ring molds, slide a spatula under the bottom of the latke-filled ring mold and use tongs to transfer the assembly to the pan. Flip the ring mold latkes using the tongs, then press down using the wine glass bottom. As the latkes are cooked, transfer them to a parchment-lined baking sheet.

TO SERVE: Place up to 3 latkes on each plate (depending on whether you're serving them as appetizers, a main course, or just want more of some of the best food Hannukah has to offer). Fold a piece of lox in half and place it on each latke. Add a dollop of the wasabi cream and a single pickled blackberry. Repeat with the remaining latkes.

NOTE: For a more formal presentation, serve the latkes with the wasabi cream and pickled blackberries, adding a rosette of thinly sliced lox, one pickled onion (page 177), and a sprinkling of edible blossoms or flowers.

ost Jews, regardless of denomination, could tell you why we eat latkes on Hanukkah, relaying the story of one day's oil lasting eight days in the Temple's Ner Tamid (the Eternal Light). Most know latkes are fried in oil in honor of that miracle and that the backstory involves a great victory by the Maccabees over the forces of Greek King Antiochus IV (215–164 BC).

The oil lasting one instead of eight days is, yes, a miracle. But the Jews prevailing over Antiochus's forces may be more so. Antiochus, to be sure, had tried to destroy us. He killed many and outlawed the practice of our religion, mandating worship of Zeus. The Maccabean Revolt cost many more lives on the way to our miraculous victory. And that's the point of the salted ash—smoky and salty and designed to not waste a scrap—on the plate in this dish, a reminder of the struggle implicit in our chosenness, of the bitterness and the pain. The red of the beets symbolizes the "Christmasization" of Hanukkah in contemporary America and the salted ash symbolizes the religious core of Hanukkah, the notion we are the Chosen People. So, once again, as it is with so many of our holidays: They tried to destroy us, we survived, let's eat!

BEET AND POTATO LATKES WITH CRÈME FRAÎCHE, CHOPPED CHIVES, AND SALTED ASH

SERVES 4 (2 LATKES PER PERSON)

FOR THE SALTED ASH:

Vegetable peelings (from various different vegetables such as those from the latkes, below)

Salt

FOR THE LATKES:

½ pound (about 2 medium) red beets, peeled and trimmed (peelings reserved for the ash)

1 medium onion, peeled and finely chopped (peelings reserved for the ash)

½ pound russet potatoes, peeled and trimmed (peelings reserved for the ash)

2 medium cloves garlic, minced

1 teaspoon salt (plus more as needed)

1 teaspoon freshly ground black pepper (plus more as needed)

TO MAKE THE SALTED ASH: Preheat oven to 350°F and line a baking sheet with parchment paper.

Place the vegetable peelings on the prepared baking sheet. Place in the oven and bake until they turn almost thoroughly to a black ash, about 1 hour. When they have ashed over and cooled, grind the resulting product in a food processor or coffee grinder. In a small bowl, combine the ash with salt in a 4:1 ratio (4 parts ash to 1 part salt), depending on how much ash is made from the charred vegetable peelings.

TO MAKE THE LATKES: While the trimmings are in the oven turning to ash, shred the beets, onion, and potatoes with the shredding disk of a food processor or on the large holes of a box grater. Transfer to a large bowl, add the garlic, salt, and pepper, and thoroughly mix. Working in batches, wrap the mixture in cheesecloth and wring the cloth until liquid flows out and the vegetables are dry. Mix in the eggs and breadcrumbs (or matzo meal) until you can form patties

2 large eggs

¼ cup breadcrumbs (or matzo meal) (plus more as needed)

Grapeseed, canola, or another neutral oil, for frying

FOR PLATING:

Crème fraîche (or Mexican crema)

Finely chopped fresh chives

that just stick together in your hands; if it is too wet, add more breadcrumbs or matzo meal 1 tablespoon at a time.

Heat ¼ inch of oil in a large heavy skillet over medium-high heat until a shred of potato immediately sizzles. Form a small amount of latke mixture into a tester disk and fry on both sides until golden brown to test for seasoning. Add more salt and pepper if needed. Form patties using 2 to 3 tablespoons, about 1 inch wide and ½ inch thick in the center, and carefully slide into the hot oil, working in batches. Fry until a golden-brown crust forms on bottom, about 3 minutes, then flip using a slotted spatula and fork and fry until golden brown on the other side and cooked through, about another 3 minutes.

TO SERVE: Using your fingers (a spoon does not work well), draw a diagonal line of salted ash across each plate from the top left corner to the bottom right corner. Place a latke on either side of the line. Spoon a dollop of crème fraîche on each latke and top with chopped chives. Diners can slide the latkes through the ash on the way toward their mouth.

Growing up, I never liked *tzimmes*, the traditional Ashkenazi stew that is usually made from carrots and dried fruits (like prunes or raisins) often combined with other sweet root vegetables like yams. It was just too sweet for me. Some cooks combined the carrot tzimmes with savory elements like beef, but, in my view, that was just confusion.

I chose to go another way, one that's more balanced among strong flavors than a dish of a single, notable sweet-sour flavor profile. I swapped the carrots out for the deep flavor (and wonderful colors) of beets and deleted the dried fruits. Beets are still a sweet vegetable but with more umami, and I added a hit of acidity and spice from the classic Mexican chile-lime spice blend Tajin. Balsamic vinegar completes the picture.

The resulting dish is a deconstructed stew that is less saucy and more about the glory of the beets. It may not look like tzimmes, but, frankly, that's a good thing. Cooking the two colors of beets separately ensures the integrity of the colors of both in the final dish.

SPICED RED AND GOLDEN BEET TZIMMES
SERVES 4 TO 6

FOR THE BALSAMIC VINEGAR REDUCTION:

1 cup balsamic vinegar

1 tablespoon Tajin (or other chile-lime-salt blend)

1 clove garlic, lightly crushed

FOR THE RED BEETS:

1 pound red beets (about 4 medium beets), peeled

2 tablespoons brown sugar

2 tablespoons honey

3 tablespoons Tajin (or other chile-lime-salt blend)

3 tablespoons grapeseed, canola, or another neutral oil

1 tablespoon balsamic vinegar

FOR THE GOLDEN BEETS:

1 pound golden beets (about 4 medium beets), peeled

2 tablespoons brown sugar

2 tablespoons honey

3 tablespoons Tajin (or other chile-lime-salt blend)

3 tablespoons grapeseed, canola, or another neutral oil

FOR THE GARNISH:

Whole parsley leaves

TO MAKE THE BALSAMIC VINEGAR REDUCTION: Put the vinegar and Tajin in a small saucepan and whisk to combine. Add the garlic and cook over medium-low heat until the vinegar has reduced until it coats the back of a spoon, about 7 to 10 minutes. This can be made ahead and refrigerated until ready to make the recipe.

TO MAKE THE BEETS: Add 2 cups water to each of two medium pots, one for each color beet. Quarter the beets lengthwise, then cut each quarter in half and add them to each pot with the brown sugar, honey, Tajin, and oil. To the red beets, add the 1 tablespoon vinegar. Bring both just to a boil over high heat, then reduce heat and simmer, stirring occasionally, until the beets are tender, about 1 hour. Discard any remaining liquid.

TO SERVE: Divide the red and yellow beets as desired among plates, drizzle with the balsamic vinegar reduction, and garnish with the parsley.

sraeli couscous may be Israeli, but it's definitely not couscous. Couscous is ground semolina (crucially without being mixed with either egg or water) rubbed together with wet hands until tiny granules form and are then dried. Israeli couscous, on the other hand, is tiny balls (about the size of larger peppercorns) of true pasta made from both wheat flour and semolina then toasted.

Asparagus is a natural mate to Israeli couscous. Its brightness and astringency pairs well with the earthiness of the pasta. Tomato confit completes the picture by bringing sweetness, acidity, and color to the dish.

ISRAELI COUSCOUS WITH ASPARAGUS AND TOMATO CONFIT

SERVES 4

1 tablespoon extra-virgin olive oil

1 cup Israeli couscous

Salt

2 to 3 cups Vegetable Stock (page 154)

14 ounces slender asparagus spears, trimmed, cut diagonally into ¾-inch pieces (about 2½ cups)

¼ cup Tomato Confit (page 193)

In a medium heavy saucepan, heat the olive oil over medium heat until shimmering. Add the Israeli couscous, season with salt, and cook until most of the couscous is golden brown, about 5 minutes. Add 2 cups of the vegetable stock, increase the heat to high, and bring to boil. Reduce the heat to medium-low, cover, and simmer until the stock is fully absorbed and the couscous is tender, about 10 minutes, adding more broth by the tablespoonful if the couscous is not yet tender.

Meanwhile, bring 4 cups of salted water to a boil in a large saucepan. Prepare an ice bath. When the water boils, add the asparagus segments and blanch until their color brightens, 3 to 4 minutes depending on the thickness of the asparagus. Remove the asparagus from the water and shock in the ice bath to fix the color. Drain and pat with paper towels to remove excess water.

Toss the asparagus with the couscous and divide into four bowls. Top each bowl with 1 tablespoon of the tomato confit and drizzle with as much as a teaspoon of oil from the confit (depending on how saucy the confit is).

created this dish somewhat late in the process of writing this book and very late one night after the arrival of a much-delayed flight from Tampa. I thought I was just throwing together a bunch of materials I had on hand from working on other dishes in this book. They made sense together.

As I plated it, though, I realized its similarity to a dish from a cookbook I'd seen the day before in Florida (*Thug Kitchen*). I added scallion salt to introduce an herbal element. While two different types of soy sauce might seem unnecessarily fussy, they each play an important role in the dish. A Cantonese chef friend of mine explained the differing roles of the two in Cantonese cooking—the light soy sauce is there for flavor more than color; with the dark it's the other way around—and it's a lesson I apply well beyond the four corners of that cuisine.

FRIED CHICKPEAS WITH TAHINI SAUCE, POACHED EGG, AND SCALLION SALT

SERVES 4

½ cup Tahini Sauce (page 159)

1 tablespoon unseasoned rice vinegar

2 teaspoons light soy sauce

1 tablespoon extra-virgin olive oil

2 (15-ounce) cans chickpeas, drained and patted dry with paper towels

2 tablespoons fresh lemon juice

1 teaspoon pomegranate molasses (or 3 teaspoons of pomegranate juice reduced to 1 teaspoon)

1 teaspoon dark soy sauce

4 tablespoons Baharat Spice Blend (page 183)

½ teaspoon Aleppo pepper (or cayenne pepper)

4 Poached Eggs (page 189)

2 tablespoons Scallion Salt (page 184)

Combine the tahini sauce, vinegar, and 1 teaspoon of the light soy sauce in the bowl of a food processor and process to a smooth, sauce-like texture.

Heat the olive oil in a large sauté pan over medium-high. Add the chickpeas and fry them until they just begin to darken, 3 to 5 minutes.

Meanwhile, in a small bowl, whisk together the lemon juice, pome-granate syrup, the remaining 1 teaspoon light soy sauce, and the dark soy sauce. Add them to the pan, stir to combine, and cook until the liquid evaporates, about 30 seconds. Stir in the Baharat spice blend and Aleppo pepper and cook for another 30 seconds. Remove the pan from the heat.

Spoon 3 tablespoons of the tahini sauce in each bowl and spread to cover the bottom of the bowl. Top the tahini with a mound (about ¼ cup) of the chickpeas. Top each plate with a poached egg and sprinkle the scallion salt over the entire plate using a cake duster.

ickled fish may be an Ashkenazi classic, but it was on a trip to Scandinavia when I really became utterly sold on the brilliance of pickled fish. This dish is a riff on one created by Chef Amy DiBiase at Vistal restaurant in San Diego. Horseradish cream pays homage to the Ashkenazi roots and amba sauce is a nod to New Israeli cuisine.

PICKLED HALIBUT WITH PERSIAN CUCUMBERS, AMBA SAUCE, AND HORSERADISH CREAM

SERVES 4

FOR THE PICKLED FISH:

1 cup salt

2 pounds halibut (or cod) fillets, cut into ½-inch pieces

⅓ cup sugar

2 cups apple cider vinegar (or white wine vinegar)

1 teaspoon yellow mustard seeds

1 teaspoon coriander seeds

2 teaspoons whole allspice

2 teaspoons black peppercorns

Peel of 1 lemon, sliced, with white pith removed

2 bay leaves

1 medium red onion, thinly sliced

FOR THE HORSERADISH CREAM:

½ cup sour cream

½ cup crème fraîche (or Mexican crema)

½ cup prepared horseradish (or freshly grated horseradish mixed with 1 tablespoon white vinegar)

1 tablespoon fresh lemon juice

Salt

FOR THE PERSIAN CUCUMBERS:

4 Persian cucumbers

Salt

FOR PLATING:

Amba (Pickled Mango) Sauce (page 165)

Rosemary flowers or other edible flowers

TO MAKE THE PICKLED FISH: Bring 4 cups water to a boil in a medium pot and whisk the salt until it is dissolved. Set aside to cool. Once the brine is cool to the touch, transfer to a container, submerge the fish pieces in it, cover, and refrigerate overnight.

The next day, combine the sugar, vinegar, mustard seeds, coriander seeds, allspice, peppercorns, and 1 cup water in a medium pot and bring to a boil over high heat. Reduce the heat and simmer for 5 minutes. Allow the pickling liquid to steep as it cools. Meanwhile, place the fish pieces in a sanitized 1-quart glass pickling jar with the sliced lemon peel, bay leaves, and red onion. Pour the cooled pickling liquid (with all the spices) over the contents, place the lid on the jar, screw on the rings, and transfer to the refrigerator overnight. The pickle will continue to improve for as much as 10 days if unopened. Store, refrigerated, for up to 1 month.

TO MAKE THE HORSERADISH CREAM: The next day (the day after you started), in a large bowl, whisk together the sour cream, crème fraîche, horseradish, and lemon juice until fully combined. Season with salt. Transfer the bowl to the refrigerator and chill for at least 1 hour, preferably 2 to 3 hours. It can be made ahead and refrigerated in a tightly sealed container for 2 to 3 weeks (though it loses flavor after a day or so).

TO MAKE THE PERSIAN CUCUMBERS: Cut the cucumber in half lengthwise, then cut into oblong segments. Place the cucumber segments in a colander, sprinkle with about a tablespoon of salt, and let them macerate for 20 minutes; then, rinse the cucumbers and pat them with a paper towel.

TO SERVE: Drizzle the amba sauce across four small plates. Remove the pickled halibut from the jar (brush off any herbs or spices) and divide amongst the plates. Repeat with the salted cucumber and, using a squeeze bottle or spoon, dollop the horseradish cream around the plate. Garnish with edible flowers.

Kibbeh is a dish of bulgur and minced meat common throughout the Middle East. The outer shell is a blend of the grain and meat, and the core is, essentially, a meatball. I first encountered the dish in my backyard, El Cajon, California. The town is one of the major landing destinations of Iraqi expatriates of both Muslim and Christian faiths.

Kibbeh is often served with a yogurt-based sauce. The laws of kashrut, of course, prohibit that, so I paired it with a sauce based on a classic Southern California ingredient those Iraqi expats surely encountered in my neck of the woods: avocado. I combined that avocado with cucumber to mimic the creamy, cooling features of the yogurt, and the dill adds a fresh, herbaceous element.

LAMB KIBBEH WITH CUCUMBER, DILL, AND AVOCADO SAUCE

SERVES 4 TO 6

FOR THE KIBBEH SHELL:

1¼ cups fine bulgur wheat (#1 or "fine" grade)

1 teaspoon salt (plus more for soaking the bulgur)

1 cup minced onion (about 1 medium onion)

1 pound ground lamb

1 teaspoon ground cumin

Freshly ground black pepper

FOR THE KIBBEH FILLING:

2 tablespoons extra-virgin olive oil

3 cloves garlic, minced

1 large yellow onion, minced

¾ pound ground lamb

¼ cup Red Meat Shawarma Spice Blend (page 183)

Salt and freshly ground black pepper

¼ cup chopped pistachios

2 tablespoons black currants

Grapeseed, canola, or another neutral oil, for frying

FOR THE AVOCADO SAUCE:

½ cup diced ripe avocado (from about ½ large avocado)

½ cup peeled and chopped Persian cucumber (about 2 Persian cucumbers)

1 tablespoon minced fresh dill

TO MAKE THE KIBBEH SHELL: Soak the bulgur in a bowl filled with warm salted water for 10 minutes. Drain off any water that hasn't been absorbed. Put the onion in the bowl of a food processor and pulse several times. Add the soaked bulgur, salt, lamb, cumin, and pepper to taste and pulse several more times to combine, then process on high speed until a paste forms, about 30 seconds.

TO MAKE THE KIBBEH FILLING: Heat the olive oil in a large sauté pan over medium-high heat. Add the garlic and onion and cook, stirring, until softened, about 5 minutes. Add the lamb and shawarma spice blend, season with salt and pepper, and cook, stirring, until the lamb is cooked through and browned, about 10 minutes. Add the pistachios and currants and cook for 2 minutes more. Remove from the heat.

TO FORM THE KIBBEH: Using your hands, form 2 tablespoons of the kibbeh shell mixture into a disk, approximately 3 inches across. Place 1 tablespoon of the filling into the center of the disk and mold the shell around it, forming the kibbeh into a football shape. Repeat with remaining shell mixture and filling.

TO MAKE THE AVOCADO SAUCE: Combine the avocado, cucumber, dill, lemon juice, and agave syrup in a high-speed blender or food processor and process until you achieve a very smooth sauce with a light green color. Taste the sauce and adjust the seasoning by adding salt and/or lemon juice as needed.

TO FRY THE KIBBEH: Pour oil into a heavy pot or Dutch oven to a depth of 2 inches. Heat over medium-high heat until a deep-fry thermometer reads 325°F. Working in batches, fry the kibbeh until

2 tablespoons fresh lemon juice
(plus more as needed)

½ teaspoon agave syrup
(or pure maple syrup)

Salt

FOR THE GARNISH:

Sumac powder

Fresh microgreens and flowers
(optional)

golden brown, turning them once, about 5 minutes. Transfer to a paper towel–lined plate.

TO SERVE: Spoon a broad swipe of the avocado sauce on each plate. Top with three kibbeh per plate and garnish with a sprinkling of sumac.

LARGE
PLATES

love dumplings! From my first Chef Boyardee ravioli to weekly Chinese dim sum outings, I've always enjoyed stuffed dumplings of just about every kind. There are few cultures that don't have their own variations on the theme. The Russian (Siberian originally) take is pelmeni. They are roughly ear-shaped dumplings that supposedly originated as a way of preserving meat during long Siberian winters. If you can manage to find premade (generally frozen) kosher pelmeni, it definitely would not be a crime to take that shortcut.

While often lumped in with Polish pierogi and Ukrainian *varenyky*, pelmeni probably are more closely related to Chinese *jiaozi*. Here, I chose to take them back in a more Polish direction using my wife's family's traditional sauerkraut and porcini filling for pierogi. I paired that with a spinach and dill broth that both complements and contrasts with the dumplings in flavor and color. The lemon zest and Korean chile threads not only add a touch of elegance to the dish but elevate it with a bit of a culinary fireworks show with their little hits of acid and heat.

The optional sauerkraut powder garnish can be made by dehydrating store-bought (or if you're really ambitious, homemade) sauerkraut in a dehydrator (or the lowest temperature on your oven) and then grinding it to a powder in a high-speed blender. It's just a garnish in this dish, but the use of sauerkraut in a second, different way on the plate really underlines what the dish is about. This recipe makes about thirty pelmeni (depending on size and efficiency of use of the dough); any leftover pelmeni can be frozen for another meal (or a late-night snack).

PELMENI OF SAUERKRAUT AND PORCINI MUSHROOMS WITH SPINACH AND DILL BROTH

SERVES 6 TO 8

FOR THE FILLING:

2 ounces dried porcini mushrooms

1 pound prepared sauerkraut (Ba-Tampte, Eden, or Claussen brands)

Freshly ground black pepper

2 tablespoons butter

FOR THE PELMENI:

1 teaspoon salt

1 tablespoon grapeseed, canola, or another neutral oil

3 cups all-purpose flour (plus more for kneading)

TO MAKE THE FILLING: In a small bowl, reconstitute the porcini mushrooms with ½ cup of boiling water for about 15 minutes. Place the sauerkraut in a large sauté pan and cook over medium heat until the sauerkraut begins to lose its firm texture, about 20 minutes. Remove from the pan. Drain the porcini mushrooms, finely chop them, add them to the pan with the butter, and cook for 3 minutes. Return the sauerkraut to the pan, season with salt and pepper, and continue to cook until the sauerkraut turns golden, about 20 minutes. Remove from heat and cool for 15 minutes, then transfer to the refrigerator. The filling can be made a day ahead and refrigerated until ready to use.

TO MAKE THE PELMENI DOUGH: In a large bowl, combine the salt, oil and 1 cup of water, stirring to dissolve the salt, then add the flour

(continued)

2 tablespoons grapeseed, canola,
or another neutral oil

1 medium onion, diced

1 medium carrot, diced

1 medium rib celery, diced

1 leek, white parts only, cleaned,
halved lengthwise, and thinly
sliced across

Salt

2 cloves garlic, minced

1 large potato (about 7 ounces),
peeled and diced

4 cups Chicken Stock (page 151)

2 bunches spinach, stems
removed (about 2 cups packed)

3 bunches fresh dill (stems
trimmed and reserved for another
purpose), roughly chopped

Juice of 1 to 2 lemons

FOR THE GARNISH:

Korean chile threads

Zest of 2 lemons

Sauerkraut powder (optional)

and mix until a stiff dough forms. Flour a clean work surface, transfer the dough to it, and knead until smooth, about 2 to 3 minutes; do not overwork the dough. Wrap the dough in plastic wrap and let it rest on the counter for at least 20 minutes and up to 2 hours.

TO MAKE THE SPINACH AND DILL BROTH: While the dough is resting, heat the oil in a large heavy-bottomed pot over medium-high heat. Add the onion, carrot, celery, and leek and cook until softened, 3 to 5 minutes. Season with salt. Add the garlic and cook until the garlic is fragrant, about 1 minute. Add the potatoes and stock, bring to a boil, then reduce the heat and simmer until the potatoes are tender, 15 to 20 minutes. Add the spinach and dill, partially cover, and cook just until they lose their texture but retain their bright color, about 1 minute. Add the juice of 1 lemon. Working in batches, carefully transfer the hot mixture to a high-speed blender and blend until smooth, transferring the broth into a clean bowl or saucepan (a food processor or immersion blender will also work, but the broth will be less smooth).

TO FORM AND COOK THE PELMENI: Transfer the sauerkraut-porcini mixture to the bowl of a food processor and pulse to combine, then process until the mixture reaches a pebbly, granular consistency, about 30 seconds.

Divide the dough into four equal portions and roll each out over a lightly floured nonstick surface to ⅛-inch thickness. Using a 3-inch biscuit or cookie cutter (or a jar top or a small glass), cut out approximately 3-inch circles of the dough and place 2 tablespoons of the filling on each circle. Recombine the scraps of dough to make additional pelmeni. Fold the edges together, creating half moon shapes, and seal, pressing tightly. Then seal the two ends of the half-moons together as well, creating the vaguely tortellini-like pelmeni shape (with the ends meeting).

In a large pot, bring 4 quarts of salted water to a boil. Working in batches, add the pelmeni and cook until they float, 3 to 5 minutes. Bring the water back to a boil before putting the next batch of pelmeni in the pot.

TO SERVE: Ladle about 1 cup of the broth into the bottom of a small soup bowl and arrange 3 pelmeni on it. Garnish with the Korean chile threads, lemon zest, and sauerkraut powder (if using). Repeat to make 6 to 8 servings.

NOTE: Depending on the exact amounts of filling and wrapper you use, there could likely be extra pelmeni beyond the 30 specified in the yield above. That is definitely not a tragedy. If there are still any left over after your meal, freeze them. Pelmeni freeze well.

rabic slang for "a mixture," shakshuka is a well-known dish throughout the Middle East and today is a core dish in modern Israeli comfort food and cuisine. Broadly speaking, shakshuka consists of eggs poached in a peppery broth of tomato, onion, and chiles. As one Israeli friend put it, "Every family has its own version and no two are alike. Shakshuka is what you make of it."

My version includes feta to amp the umami, black olives for pungency, and green *schug* for a hit of heat.

SHAKSHUKA WITH FETA AND BLACK OLIVES

SERVES 6

2 tablespoons extra-virgin olive oil

1 medium onion, finely chopped

1 leek, white parts only, cleaned, halved lengthwise, and thinly sliced across

1 bulb fennel, cored and finely chopped (fronds and stalks reserved for another purpose)

2 large red bell peppers, finely chopped

2 Fresno (or red jalapeño) chiles, stems, seeds, and ribs removed, thinly sliced

3 cloves garlic, minced

1 tablespoon Spanish sweet paprika

1 tablespoon Spanish smoked paprika

2 teaspoons ground cumin

1 (28-ounce) can whole tomatoes, crushed by hand, juice reserved

¾ cup chopped fresh parsley

6 large eggs

Salt and freshly ground black pepper

FOR THE GARNISH:

1 to 2 tablespoons crumbled feta cheese (to taste)

12 oil-cured black olives, pitted and sliced in half lengthwise

Coarse sea salt for finishing

Green Schug (page 160)

In a large pot or Dutch oven, heat the olive oil over medium heat until it is just shimmering. Add the onion, leek, fennel, bell pepper, and chiles and stir once, letting the vegetables sweat until softened but not browned, about 4 to 5 minutes. Add the garlic and cook, stirring, until fragrant, about 30 seconds. Stir in both paprikas and the cumin and cook until fragrant, about 30 seconds, then add the tomatoes and their juice and stir to combine. Reduce the heat and simmer until the flavors fully meld and the canned flavor is cooked out of the tomatoes, about 10 minutes. Add half of the parsley.

Carefully add the eggs one at a time to the simmering mixture, then cover the pot and poach until the egg whites are just set, about 9 minutes. Turn off the heat and season with salt and pepper.

To serve, ladle the shakshuka mixture into bowls and top each with a poached egg. Arrange the cheese, olives, and the remaining parsley around the eggs. Garnish with the sea salt and serve immediately with the green schug.

F alafel is one of quite a few dishes claimed as their own by both Israeli Jews and their Arab neighbors. It is, traditionally, deep-fried balls made from ground chickpeas or dried fava beans (or both) with herbs, spices, and sometimes aromatic vegetables added to the dough. In this version I feature parsley in its fresh, brilliant green form along with chickpeas and their flour. I pair that with a brilliant pink hummus for a dramatic, colorful presentation.

HERBED FALAFEL WITH BEET HUMMUS
SERVES 6

FOR THE BEET HUMMUS:

10 to 12 ounces small red beets (about 3), roasted (see page 92) and cooled

1 (15-ounce) can chickpeas, drained

Zest and juice of 1 large lemon (plus more as needed)

Salt and freshly ground black pepper

2 large cloves garlic, minced

2 heaping tablespoons tahini

¼ cup extra-virgin olive oil

FOR THE HERBED FALAFEL:

1 cup canned chickpeas, drained

¼ cup chickpea (gram) flour (plus more for coating)

½ teaspoon baking powder

1 cup chopped fresh parsley

¼ cup dried parsley

2 cloves garlic, chopped

¼ large yellow onion, chopped (about ¼ cup)

½ teaspoon salt

½ teaspoon ground cumin

Grapeseed, canola, or another neutral oil for frying

FOR THE GARNISH:

Parsley, garlic, or fennel flowers (optional)

TO MAKE THE BEET HUMMUS: Cut the beets in quarters and place them in the bowl of a food processor. Start by pulsing, and process until only small bits remain. Add the chickpeas, lemon zest and juice, salt and pepper to taste, the garlic, and tahini and process until smooth. With the machine still running, drizzle the olive oil in a slow and steady stream through the feed tube until the hummus is smooth and glossy. Taste for seasoning and adjust with more salt or lemon juice; if it is too thick, stir in lemon juice or water until you reach your desired consistency. Transfer the hummus to a bowl, cover, and refrigerate until ready to serve. Clean the food processor bowl.

TO MAKE THE HERBED FALAFEL: In the bowl of a food processor, combine the chickpeas, chickpea flour, baking powder, parsleys, garlic, onion, salt, and cumin and pulse several times, then process on high speed until smooth. Transfer the falafel mixture to a bowl. Using your hands, roll 2 tablespoons of the mixture at a time to make 12 golf ball–sized spheres.

Pour oil into a heavy pot or Dutch oven to a depth of 2 inches. Heat over medium-high heat until a deep-fry thermometer reads 350°F. Drop the first batch of falafel balls into the oil and fry until they turn a nice brown color on the outside, about 3 minutes. Using a slotted spoon, transfer the falafel to a paper towel–lined plate. Repeat until all the falafel are cooked.

TO SERVE: Cut one-third of the falafel in half, leaving the others whole. Using the back of a spoon, a spatula, or plating tool of your choice, spread a diagonal line of the beet hummus on each plate. Place two whole falafel on top of the hummus and arrange two falafel halves, cut-side up, revealing their beautiful color, on the plate. Garnish with the flowers.

nvoltini of eggplant is a classic Italian *primi* (appetizer) in which thin strips of eggplant are stuffed with ricotta, baked, and served over a classic marinara sauce; however, I think involtini can be so much more than a starter. I've reworked the dish here to make it totally vegan with "ricotta" made of pine nuts. Nutritional yeast provides rich umami. Naturally, the dish works as either an appetizer or main, depending entirely on how much you love eggplant.

INVOLTINI OF EGGPLANT AND PINE NUT "RICOTTA"

SERVES 2 AS A MAIN COURSE

FOR THE PINE NUT "RICOTTA":

1 cup pine nuts

1 tablespoon fresh lemon juice

1 tablespoon nutritional yeast

½ teaspoon salt

1 clove garlic

FOR THE INVOLTINI:

2 Italian (or Asian) eggplants (not standard American globe eggplants)

2 tablespoons extra-virgin olive oil

FOR PLATING:

¾ cup Quick Tomato Sauce (page 173)

Microgreens (such as micro basil) or fresh herb leaves (such as oregano)

TO MAKE THE PINE NUT "RICOTTA": In a large bowl, cover the pine nuts with 3 cups water and let soak until they noticeably swell and soften, 2 to 4 hours. Drain, rinse well, then transfer the pine nuts to a high-speed blender or food processor. Add the lemon juice, nutritional yeast, salt, garlic, and ¼ cup water and pulse until combined. Add more water as needed until you achieve a smooth texture.

TO MAKE THE INVOLTINI: Preheat the oven to 350°F and line a baking sheet with parchment paper.

Using a mandoline or very sharp knife, carefully slice the eggplant lengthwise into $\frac{1}{16}$- to ⅛-inch-thick strips (if too wide, trim to about ¾ inch). Discard (or, better yet, reserve for use in stock) the outside strips (the ones with skin on one side) and select the best-looking ones. You should get at least 6 to 8 good ones, depending on the size of your eggplants. Drizzle the eggplant strips on both sides with olive oil, place them on the prepared baking sheet, and roast until they begin to lose their texture, about 15 minutes.

Choose the most attractive of the eggplant strips after cooking and cut each down to about 4 inches in length. Place about a heaping tablespoon of the "ricotta" in the middle of each one and fold the eggplant over, seam-side down.

TO SERVE: To serve as an appetizer, spoon 3 tablespoons of the tomato sauce into a shallow bowl or plate and top with an involtini, seam-side down, and sprinkle with microgreens or herbs. If you wish to serve it as a main course, pour a pool of the sauce in the center of each plate. The size of the pool will depend on how many involtini you plan to serve per plate. One would be good for a small appetizer, three for a small entrée (though you'll have to triple the recipe). Top each pool with the involtini and garnish with microgreens or herbs.

Caramelized onions are the classic accompaniment for *mujadarra*, a lentils-and-rice dish of Iraqi origin popular throughout the Arab world. The dish arrived in Israel with the Jewish immigrants from Arab lands. In addition to the classic elements of lentils, rice, and caramelized onions, I add a dollop of *sofregit* of tomatoes, onions, and olive oil—the classic Catalan version of sofrito—to highlight the Sephardic connections and give the dish a bit of acidity.

Pita is a wonderful delivery device for the mujadarra. It could be used as a pocket to be filled by the dish. Or it could be used as a utensil. Either way, it helps make this a fun dish to eat.

MUJADARRA WITH CARAMELIZED ONIONS AND SOFREGIT

SERVES 4 TO 6

FOR THE MUJADARRA:

4 cups Roast Vegetable Stock (page 154)

1 cup brown lentils

1 cup long-grain white rice (preferably jasmine)

FOR THE CARAMELIZED ONIONS:

2 tablespoons extra-virgin olive oil

1 tablespoon cumin seeds

1 teaspoon cracked black peppercorns

4 medium onions, halved and sliced

1 teaspoon salt

FOR SERVING:

3 pitas

4 to 6 heaping tablespoons Sofregit (page 167)

TO MAKE THE MUJADARRA: In a large pot, bring the stock to a boil over high heat and add the lentils. Cover the pot, reduce the heat to low, and simmer for 20 minutes. Add the rice, return to a boil, then reduce the heat to low and simmer for another 20 minutes.

TO MAKE THE CARAMELIZED ONIONS: Meanwhile, in a large skillet over medium-high heat, heat the oil until it shimmers. Drop in the cumin seeds and cracked peppercorns and cook, shaking the pan, until the cumin seeds darken, about 1 minute. Add the onions and salt. Lower the heat to medium and cook, stirring frequently, until the onions turn a dark caramel brown, about 15 minutes. If the onions begin to stick to the bottom of the pan, add a little water.

TO SERVE: Cut the pitas in half. Top the mujadarra with the caramelized onions and a quenelle of sofregit. Pass the pitas for scooping or filling.

'm a devout believer in simplicity no matter how complicated it is to get there. All things being equal, I prefer the idea of fewer things on a plate: three or four, at most. This is basically two things on a plate: leek and asparagus vinaigrette. Grilling the leeks lends complexity to this simple dish. The char on the leeks not only adds color and textural interest but a layer of smoky flavor as well as a wonderful contrast of temperature to the cool asparagus vinaigrette.

GRILLED LEEKS WITH ASPARAGUS VINAIGRETTE

SERVES 4

FOR THE ASPARAGUS VINAIGRETTE:

Salt

1 pound asparagus, trimmed

½ teaspoon Dijon mustard

3 tablespoons Lemon and Red Wine Vinaigrette (page 175)

FOR THE GRILLED LEEKS:

6 small leeks, white parts only with roots attached (but carefully washed)

2 teaspoons extra-virgin olive oil

Salt

FOR THE GARNISH:

Korean chili threads (optional)

TO MAKE THE ASPARAGUS VINAIGRETTE: Bring a large pot of salted water to a boil and prepare an ice bath. Add the asparagus and blanch just until it turns a brilliant green color and is tender, 2 to 3 minutes depending on its size. Transfer the asparagus to the ice bath to stop the cooking and cool the asparagus.

Once cooled, drain, roughly chop and add the asparagus to a high-speed blender or food processor along with the mustard and lemon and red wine vinaigrette and blend to a smooth consistency.

TO GRILL THE LEEKS: Preheat a charcoal or gas grill to medium-high heat or set a grill pan over medium-high heat on the stovetop. Pour about 1 inch of water into a large pot over medium-high heat. Insert a steamer basket and set the leeks into the steamer. Cover and cook until tender when the white end is pierced with a paring knife, about 5 minutes. Remove the leeks from the steamer, pat dry, and transfer to a shallow dish.

Brush the leeks with the olive oil and season them with salt. Arrange the leeks on the grill (or grill pan) and cook without moving them until grill marks appear, about 3 minutes. Flip the leeks over and grill on the other side until grill marks appear and they're tender and give when you press them with a fork or finger, about another 3 minutes.

TO SERVE: Spoon ¼ cup of the asparagus vinaigrette onto each plate and top with 2 to 3 grilled leek halves, and garnish with the Korean chili threads (if using). To serve as an appetizer, spoon 2 tablespoons of the asparagus vinaigrette onto each plate and top with a leek half.

While I'm definitely not a vegan, I love a good vegan dish. What I look for is a celebration of vegetables and what can be done with them, not processed meat substitutes designed to be meat except for the fact they're not meat. This dish is all about the vegetables appearing in every state: raw, cooked, pickled, and fermented. There's no reason to miss meat and not because anything tastes like meat but because there's so much else to hold one's interest.

Of those supporting players the spice blend is the most important. *Baharat* is Arabic for "spices," and the exotic, aromatic, savory blend by that name has become one of the most important in Israel. Using it here helps underline the meatiness of the cauliflower.

As I was developing this recipe, I knew I wanted to cook the cauliflower whole, not in florets. The challenge, though, was figuring out how to cook it evenly so that the stem would be as edibly delicious as the tips of the florets. I found the answer in a place I should have expected it: the New York outpost (at Chelsea Market) of one of my favorite Tel Aviv restaurants: Miznon (see page 81). I ordered one of their famous roast cauliflower dishes and was pretty sure I knew how they did it. The first dish I made when I got home was this one. It worked!

BAHARAT ROAST CAULIFLOWER WITH PICKLED RED CABBAGE AND PUMPKIN SEED SAUCE

SERVES 1 TO 2

FOR THE ROAST CAULIFLOWER:

1 small head cauliflower (1½ to 2 pounds)

1 teaspoon salt (plus more for boiling the cauliflower)

3 tablespoons extra-virgin olive oil

½ teaspoon Baharat Spice Blend (page 183)

TO MAKE THE ROAST CAULIFLOWER: Preheat the oven to 400°F and line a baking sheet with parchment paper.

Trim the base of the cauliflower just enough so that it can stand upright. If possible, try to keep some of the leaves at the base of the cauliflower. They look cool. Pour enough water into a medium pot (just large enough to fit the cauliflower head with a bit of room to spare) so that it comes 1 inch up the sides (about 1 quart of water). Add salt and whisk to combine. Bring to a boil over high heat. Carefully stand the cauliflower head in the pot (stem-side down) and cover. Steam until the florets are just barely tender and the cauliflower is no longer pearly white in color, 10 to 12 minutes. Remove the cauliflower from the pot using a metal spoon and set aside. Let the cauliflower cool for about 10 minutes.

While the cauliflower is cooling, in a small bowl, whisk together the olive oil, Baharat spice blend, and salt. Spoon the spiced oil over the

(continued)

FOR THE PUMPKIN SEED SAUCE:

⅓ cup green pepitas (pumpkin seeds)

1 tablespoon apple cider vinegar

1 teaspoon fresh lime juice (plus more as needed)

½ teaspoon onion powder

1 teaspoon sea salt (plus more as needed)

1 clove garlic, peeled

1 Persian cucumber, chopped

2 tablespoons nutritional yeast

1 teaspoon white (shiro) miso

Freshly ground black pepper

2 tablespoons chopped fresh parsley leaves

FOR THE ACCOMPANIMENT:

Pickled Red Cabbage (page 177)

cauliflower and transfer it to the prepared baking sheet. Transfer the baking sheet to the oven and roast until golden brown all over (with some bits slightly charred), 20 to 30 minutes.

TO MAKE THE PUMPKIN SEED SAUCE: While the cauliflower is roasting, combine the pepitas, vinegar, lime juice, onion powder, salt, garlic, cucumber, nutritional yeast, miso, pepper to taste, parsley, and ¼ cup water in the bowl of a high-speed blender or food processor and, starting on low (and gradually increasing), blend until it's a completely smooth purée. Taste the resulting sauce for seasoning and adjust accordingly with lime juice or salt.

TO SERVE: Pour a pool of the pumpkin seed sauce in the bottom of a wide, shallow bowl. Place the whole roast cauliflower head in the bowl and top with the pickled cabbage. This dish is designed to be shared by two, each of whom should feel free to attack the cauliflower with abandon. Of course, there's no reason not to keep it all for yourself and make a second one for the would-have-been sharer.

F ish cakes—aka "gefilte fish"—aren't just for Passover anymore. And gefilte fish aren't just a tradition honored as much in the dreading as the eating. They don't have to come out of that roundly reviled bottle with the orange label, and they don't have to be a bad joke told once a year.

Once upon a time gefilte fish were, in fact, a great glory of Ashkenazi cuisine. *Gefilte* translates as "stuffed" and, originally, gefilte fish were (as the name suggests) fish stuffed with ground fish, bound by their own collagen (and sometimes matzo meal, another premodern culinary tour de force). But midcentury American technology and industry—and its tendency to exchange convenience for quality and deliciousness—eventually turned gefilte fish into a sad punch line of a dish.

This recipe not only reverses that course but substitutes a bit of contemporary elegance for the seemingly antiquated style of the traditional dish. The star of this version is gorgeous orange steelhead trout. It's one of America's most readily available freshwater (at least partially) fish with an elegant, rich, salmon-like flavor. Herbs (blanched to brighten their color), mustard, and a contemporary presentation complete the picture.

STEELHEAD TROUT CAKES WITH HERBED MUSTARD (GEFILTE FISH 1)

SERVES 4 AS A MAIN DISH OR 6 TO 8 AS AN APPETIZER

FOR THE TROUT CAKES:

2 tablespoons extra-virgin olive oil

1 medium onion, chopped

1 medium carrot, chopped

1 bulb fennel, cored and chopped (fronds and stalks reserved for another purpose)

2 roasted red peppers, skinned and chopped (if using jarred, rinse before using)

2 pounds steelhead trout fillets (see note)

Kosher salt and freshly ground black pepper

½ teaspoon Spanish sweet paprika

TO MAKE THE TROUT CAKES: In a large sauté pan, heat the olive oil over low heat. Add the onion, carrot, and fennel and sweat just until translucent, about 2 minutes. Transfer to the bowl of a food processor and add the roasted red peppers and fish. Season with salt and black pepper, and the paprika and process to roughly uniform consistency. Fry up a small sample of the resulting cake mixture, taste for seasoning, and adjust accordingly.

Place an 8-inch piece of aluminum foil on a cutting board. Leaving a generous margin of foil around it on all sides and using one third of the fish mixture, spoon a 2- to 3-inch line (1 to 1½ inches wide) horizontally along the middle of the foil and roll it up into a cylindrical shape, pinching the ends to seal. Next, place a slightly larger piece of plastic wrap on the cutting board and roll around the wrapped fish, forming a roulade. Use the plastic wrap to ensure your roll is tight by twisting the ends in opposite directions. When you have a secure, tight roulade, tie off the ends with kitchen twine. Repeat twice more until all the fish mixture is used.

(continued)

FOR THE HERBED MUSTARD:

2 tablespoons chopped fresh parsley leaves

2 tablespoons chopped fresh dill

2 tablespoons chopped fresh basil

½ cup Dijon mustard

FOR THE GARNISH:

Red Pepper Skin Curls (page 196; optional)

Microgreens (optional)

Finishing salt (if not using the red pepper skin curls, a red salt would be nice)

Bring a large pot of water to a boil and turn the heat down to a bare simmer. Place the roulades in the pot and cook for 10 minutes. Remove the roulades from the water and allow them to rest on the counter to cool for 15 minutes. Transfer to the refrigerator and chill for at least 30 minutes up to overnight. Transfer to a cutting board, unwrap the fish sausage, and slice into 1-inch cylindrical sections.

TO MAKE THE HERBED MUSTARD: While the roulades are cooking, bring a small pot of water to a boil and prepare an ice bath in a large bowl. Plunge the herbs into the water to blanch just to fix the brilliant green color, about 10 seconds. Immediately shock in the ice bath to stop the cooking (and preserve the color; see Herb Oil, page 191), then squeeze dry. Place the herbs in the bowl of a food processor along with the mustard and process until fully combined.

TO SERVE: This dish can work either as an appetizer or a main. For an elegant presentation, place two 1-tablespoon dollops of the herbed mustard at the center of the plate, one beside the other. Swipe the dollop on the left diagonally toward the upper right corner of the plate and then the dollop on the right diagonally toward the lower right corner of the plate. Center a cylindrical section of the trout cake roulade over the two dollops and top with a few curls of julienned red pepper skins (if using). There is nothing wrong with plating the dish more simply—a couple tablespoons of herbed mustard topped by a roulade and garnished with the pepper curls, microgreens and/or finishing salt. For a heartier portion dollop 2 tablespoons of the herbed mustard in the center of a plate and arrange 3 roulades on it, garnishing each.

NOTE: Steelhead trout is, genetically, identical to rainbow trout. Indeed, most fisheries in America's west treat them as a single species who just choose to live their lives differently (like many siblings). While rainbows live their days in fresh water only, steelheads spend time in both fresh water and salt water. This dish, then, is a bit of an homage to the Ashkenazi tradition, updated based on the best readily available product.

Gefilte fish is, of course, a classic Ashkenazi Passover dish. This version, in addition to being a different contemporary take on the classic—capturing the essential goodness of the original—is also a retelling of the entire story of the Exodus on a plate.

Scallions were and remain one of the most commonly grown vegetables in Egypt. The pickling in this dish reflects the sourness of the ancient Jews' status as slaves. Conversely, fava beans were and still are one of the most commonly grown vegetables in Israel. Thus, the dish reflects travel from the scallions of Egypt, on the top, to the fava beans of Israel, on the bottom. In between is—of course—the Red Sea, which is represented by one of the most common fish found therein: grouper.

It is perfectly acceptable to use good-quality pickled shallots (which can, for example, be purchased at nearly any Asian market) in place of the scallions. However, with a little planning, it is also not difficult to make excellent pickled scallions. This recipe will make more tomato-saffron oil than you will need for this dish. Both keep well and can be deployed for many other uses. The beautiful orange oil could be an excellent garnish for, among other dishes in this book, the Short Rib Goulash (page 87) or the Aushak with Duxelles (page 126).

GROUPER QUENELLES WITH FAVA BEAN PURÉE AND PICKLED SCALLIONS (GEFILTE FISH 2)

MAKES 8

FOR THE TOMATO-SAFFRON OIL:

1 tablespoon saffron (or safflower) threads

2 small tomatoes, chopped

1½ cups canola oil

FOR THE FAVA BEAN PURÉE:

2 cups Chicken Stock (page 151)

2 cups double-peeled fava beans (fresh or frozen and thawed)

½ cup white wine vinegar

TO MAKE THE TOMATO-SAFFRON OIL: Combine the saffron, tomatoes, and canola oil in a medium saucepan, bring to a simmer over medium heat, and simmer for 30 minutes to infuse. Remove from the heat. When the oil is fully cooled, spoon off the orange oil at the top and pour through a funnel topped with a fine-mesh sieve into a squeeze bottle. Discard the solids.

TO MAKE THE FAVA BEAN PURÉE: In a medium saucepan, bring the stock to a boil over high heat. Transfer to the bowl of a high-speed blender or food processor, add the fava beans and vinegar, and process until you achieve a smooth texture, scraping the sides of the bowl occasionally, as needed.

FOR THE GROUPER GEFILTE FISH:

1 large white onion, chopped

2 large carrots, chopped

2 ribs celery, chopped

1 tablespoon grapeseed, canola, or another neutral oil

2 pounds grouper (or halibut or cod) fillets, cut into 1-inch pieces

1 egg white

Grapeseed, canola, or another neutral oil, for cooking the fish cakes

FOR THE GARNISH:

16 pieces of Pickled Scallions (page 178)

TO MAKE THE GROUPER GEFILTE FISH: Sweat the onion, carrots, and celery in the oil in a sauté pan until just translucent, about 2 minutes. Working in batches, process the mirepoix, grouper, and egg white in the bowl of a food processor until fully combined into a relatively smooth paste. Oil the insides of four 3-inch ring molds (an emptied tuna can with the bottom cut off can work, too) and fill with about 1 inch of the grouper purée. Use the bottom of a wine glass to press the purée into a relatively solid mass.

Heat a large sauté pan with just enough oil to very lightly coat over medium heat. Transfer the ring molds with the grouper purée to the pan, remove the ring molds using tongs, and cook until they are just beginning to caramelize on the bottom, about 2 to 3 minutes. Flip the gefilte fish cakes and cook for another 2 to 3 minutes, until cooked through. Repeat with the remaining grouper purée.

TO SERVE: Spoon about 2 tablespoons of the fava bean purée into soup bowls or dishes and spread in a circular pattern. Center a fish cake on top of the purée and top with 2 pickled scallions. Line the outside of the purée with the tomato-saffron oil.

Knishes, the classic Eastern European snack of a filling—most frequently ground meat and mashed potatoes—wrapped in dough and either deep-fried or baked is one of the world's great comfort foods. But while meat and/or potato fillings are most common for knishes, there's no reason it couldn't be something different if, in its own right, equally loved.

One of my Jewish deli favorites has always been smoked whitefish. The smoky flavor works perfectly on salads or bagels, but why not take it in a different classic Jewish deli direction? If it wasn't already traditional knish filling, my question was: Why not? The lightness of the smoked whitefish filling elevates the dish (which, frankly, would be excellent with any good-quality smoked fish from your local fishmonger or Jewish deli).

SMOKED WHITEFISH KNISHES

MAKES ABOUT 8 MEDIUM KNISHES

FOR THE KNISH DOUGH:

2½ cups all-purpose flour (plus more for dusting)

1 teaspoon baking powder

½ teaspoon kosher salt

1 large whole egg

½ cup grapeseed, canola, or another neutral oil

1 teaspoon distilled vinegar

1 egg yolk

FOR THE FILLING:

2 large potatoes (about 8 ounces each), cut into 1-inch-thick slices

⅓ cup Chicken Stock (page 151)

1 tablespoon fresh thyme leaves

½ teaspoon kosher salt

½ teaspoon freshly ground black pepper

¼ pound smoked whitefish (or other good-quality smoked fish), finely flaked

FOR PLATING:

4 Poached Eggs (page 189; optional)

Hot sauce (optional)

Leaves from 1 sprig thyme

Finishing salt

TO MAKE THE KNISH DOUGH: Stir the flour, baking powder, and kosher salt into a large bowl. In another bowl, whisk together the egg, oil, vinegar, and ½ cup water, pour over the dry ingredients, and stir to combine. Once the mixture is a craggy, uneven mass, knead until smooth, about 1 minute. You can also do this in a food processor. Place the dough back in the bowl and cover with plastic wrap. Set aside at room temperature for 1 hour (or in the fridge for up to 3 days).

TO FILL AND BAKE THE KNISHES: Preheat oven to 375°F and line a large baking sheet with parchment paper.

Place the potatoes in a medium saucepan and cover with water. Bring to a boil over medium-high heat, then reduce the heat and simmer for 15 minutes, or until tender. Drain the potatoes and transfer to a large bowl. Add the stock, thyme, kosher salt, pepper, and smoked whitefish and mash until well combined.

If your dough has sweated some beads of oil while resting, knead it to reincorporate. Divide dough in half; set one half aside. On a well-floured surface, roll the first half into a very thin sheet (roughly an 8 x 8-inch square about ⅛ inch thick). Cut the dough into rounds 3 inches in diameter. Because the dough will be elastic and spring back, pull it a little to stretch it again. Place 1 tablespoon of the filling in the center of each round, then fold over and pinch the edges together to firmly seal them. Repeat with the remaining dough and filling.

Arrange the knishes on the prepared baking sheet with a little space between them. Whisk the egg yolk and a ½ cup water together to form a glaze and brush it over the knish dough. Bake the knishes for about 45 minutes, rotating the sheet if needed for them to bake into an even golden brown color.

TO SERVE: Place a knish in the center of each plate. Top each knish with a poached egg (if using). Sprinkle some hot sauce (if using) on top of each egg and garnish with thyme leaves and finishing salt.

oast chicken is one of those classics that has a place in both the restaurant and home kitchen. Many (if not most) great chefs from the Western traditions wax effusive about roast chicken. It's a dish they see as the test of a great cook, the dish they make at home and a fitting choice for a favorite dish. It is just that for my wife and me. It's our perfect date night at home, romantic dinner. There's no better way to slide into the weekend on a Friday night than to share a beautifully crispy-skinned roast bird.

Many great recipes for roast chicken have the cook rubbing its skin, inside and out, with butter. That, of course, doesn't work in the kosher kitchen. But why, I wondered, would one even want to use butter when the chicken's own fat is so tasty? Chill the schmaltz so it's solid, massage it into slits in the chicken's skin, and that schmaltz will add richness to the chicken throughout. If it's not exactly a chicken confit—and it's not—in some ways it acts as if it were.

This dish absolutely doesn't need a sauce, though Mayonnaise (page 168) is a delicious dipping-sauce accompaniment. In fact, the earliest written records of mayonnaise are as an accompaniment to chicken. A good alternative to the lentils would be to chop a variety of root vegetables, season them up, set the bird to roast on top of them, and let the schmaltzy chicken juices permeate the veggies with flavor.

ROAST CHICKEN WITH SCHMALTZ MASSAGE AND LE PUY LENTILS

SERVES 2

FOR THE CHICKEN:

1 whole chicken (about 3 pounds)

Salt and freshly ground black pepper

2 shallots, halved

1 large carrot, roughly chopped

8 to 10 sprigs thyme

2 to 3 tablespoons Schmaltz (page 187), depending on the exact size of the bird (straight out of the refrigerator so that it is solid, not liquid)

1 lemon, cut in half

TO MAKE THE CHICKEN: If you can manage to think ahead in the course of your daily life—as dedicated to food as I may be, I rarely manage to do so—season the chicken both inside and out with salt and pepper one to two days ahead of time and refrigerate until ready to cook. This technique—pioneered by Judy Rodgers of Zuni Café—is basically a dry brine. If, like the rest of us, you do not manage to do so, know that you can still end up with a delicious chicken by salting it as close as possible to the time it goes into the oven.

Set a rack in the middle of the oven and preheat the oven to 450°F.

If you haven't pre-salted the chicken, do so now on the inside—not the outside. Stuff the cavity with the shallots, carrot, and thyme and truss the chicken.

Lift up the skin from the breasts of the chicken and spoon 1 tablespoon of schmaltz onto the breasts. You may need to cut a tiny slit where the skin meets the flesh. Massage the breasts to spread the

(continued)

FOR THE LENTILS:

1 small onion

3 whole cloves

1 cup Le Puy lentils (or beluga lentils), picked over and rinsed

1 medium carrot, trimmed and cut into 4 pieces

1 rib celery, trimmed and cut into 4 pieces

1 bay leaf

2 cups Chicken Stock (page 151)

schmaltz evenly. Flip the chicken and do the same with another tablespoon of schmaltz on the other side.

Place the chicken on a wire rack fitted into a roasting pan, breast-side up. Squeeze about half the juice of the lemon over the chicken and season with salt and pepper. Flip the bird and do the same on the other side. Place the bird in the oven, breast-side down, and cook for 20 minutes.

Turn the oven temperature down to 375°F. Pull the bird from the oven and flip it so the breast side is facing up. In my experience the best way to flip a bird in mid-cook (with juices in the pan and all) is to carefully grab the bird using tongs in one hand and a spatula in your other hand to help turn the bird (without ripping the skin). Return the bird to the oven and cook for another 40 minutes, until the skin is golden brown. An instant-read thermometer inserted into a meaty part of the leg (avoiding the bone) should register 165°F.

TO MAKE THE LENTILS: About 20 minutes into the final cooking of the chicken, stud the onion with the cloves, place in a large sauce-pan, and add the lentils, carrot, celery, bay leaf, and chicken stock. Bring to a boil over high heat, then turn the heat down and simmer, uncovered, until substantially all of the water is absorbed and the lentils are tender, about 25-30 minutes.

TO FINISH AND SERVE: Remove the chicken from the oven and transfer to a cutting board to rest for 10 minutes. When the lentils are done, remove the onion, carrot, and celery and scoop the lentils into the center of a platter. It is entirely your choice whether to cut up the chicken or serve it, magnificently, whole. Top the lentils with the chicken and let the chicken's juices run into the lentils.

Mindfulness and respect are at the core of kosher cuisine. Using the non-glory cuts of meat is at the essence of respecting the beasts that feed us. This dish celebrates one of the un-fancied parts of poultry: the liver. And if we ask an animal to give its life to feed us, there is something profoundly wrong about sending significant portions of it to a landfill.

From a purely hedonistic point of view, grilling chicken livers has the distinct benefit of yielding a marvelously caramelized exterior and a luxuriously creamy interior. The acidity (and spice) of the parsley-lemon sauce cuts through the buttery richness of the livers. If serving as an appetizer instead of a main course, use more skewers with fewer livers on each.

GRILLED CHICKEN LIVERS WITH PARSLEY-LEMON SAUCE

SERVES 2 TO 4

FOR THE CHICKEN LIVER SKEWERS:

1 pound chicken livers, trimmed

Salt and freshly ground black pepper

FOR THE PARSLEY-LEMON SAUCE:

¼ cup fresh parsley leaves

½ cup finely chopped red onion

1 to 2 teaspoons red chiles flakes (to taste)

⅓ cup fresh lemon juice

1 tablespoon light soy sauce

1 teaspoon Worcestershire sauce

2 tablespoons dry sherry

1 anchovy fillet, rinsed

TO ASSEMBLE THE SKEWERS: Soak wooden skewers in hot water for at least 1 hour prior to use. Prepare and start the grill as necessary and appropriate to your setup, setting it to moderate heat. Thread the livers onto skewers, using two skewers for each set of livers. This gives you more control of them as they cook. Leave a little space on the skewers between the livers. Season the livers with salt and black pepper.

TO MAKE THE PARSLEY-LEMON SAUCE: Combine the parsley, onion, red chile flakes, lemon juice, soy sauce, Worcestershire sauce, sherry, and anchovy in a high-speed blender or food processor and blend until a smooth texture is achieved. Refrigerate the resulting sauce for at least 30 minutes and up to an hour before using to allow the flavors to fully combine.

TO COOK THE LIVERS AND SERVE: Grill the livers over moderate heat (indirect heat is best), turning once, until just charred outside and still slightly pink within, about 5 minutes.

Carefully remove the chicken livers from the skewers. Pour a circular pool of sauce at the center of your plates and arrange the chicken livers in a diagonal stripe from the bottom left of the plate to the top right on top of the sauce (the number of livers per serving depends on whether the dish is being served as an appetizer or a main course).

One of Mexico's favorite tacos is made from fried *chicharrones* (pork skin) rehydrated by stewing in a tasty salsa, whether red or green. What's good for pork skin may be better with *gribenes*, that classic Ashkenazi treatment of chicken skin. While gribenes are traditionally prized for their crispy texture, this dish takes them in a different direction; one that explores other textural possibilities (much as chicharrones are explored in the classic Mexican preparations). They're all the better for it.

TACOS OF GRIBENES IN SALSA VERDE

SERVES 4 TO 6

FOR THE TACOS:

1½ pounds fresh tomatillos (about 8, depending on size), husks removed

4 fresh poblano chiles

2 fresh jalapeño chiles

1 tablespoon Schmaltz (page 187)

1 large onion, chopped

3 cloves garlic, crushed

Salt and freshly ground black pepper

½ to 1 cup Chicken Stock (page 151)

1½ teaspoons dried oregano

½ cup fresh cilantro leaves, coarsely chopped

2 cups Gribenes (page 187)

12 corn tortillas, recipe follows

FOR THE ACCOMPANIMENTS:

Pickled Red Cabbage (page 177)

Fried shallots (optional)

Roasted Tomato, Arbol Chile, and Garlic Salsa (page 172)

Set a rack 6 inches below the heat source and preheat the broiler. Line a baking sheet with parchment paper.

Arrange the tomatillos on the prepared sheet, place them in the broiler, and broil until their surfaces are lightly browned and, where they're still green, are slightly translucent. Meanwhile, holding the poblano and jalapeño chiles with tongs or suspending them on a grate over a stovetop gas burner (or, on a sauté pan if your stove's burners are electric), set to medium heat and roast the chiles, flipping them to their other surfaces when their skin blackens over. When all surfaces of the chiles are evenly blackened, place them in plastic bags, tie off the bags, and let them steam until the blackened surfaces begin to separate from the flesh of the chiles, about 5 minutes. Once the chiles have cooled, using your hands (not knives and not running water), rub the blackened skins off the flesh of the chiles. Be careful not to touch your eyes.

Combine the schmaltz, onion, and garlic in a medium sauté pan, season with salt and pepper, and sweat over medium heat until the vegetables give up their water. Add ½ cup of the stock and bring to a boil. Lower the heat and simmer for 5 minutes.

Add the contents of the sauté pan, the chiles, tomatillos, oregano, cilantro, and 1 to 2 teaspoons salt to a high-speed blender or food processor and blend until thoroughly puréed. Taste the sauce and adjust both the texture and seasoning, if necessary, by adding additional stock and/or salt.

Combine the salsa verde sauce and gribenes in a large saucepan and bring to a boil over medium-high heat. Turn down the heat and cook until the gribenes are warm and soft, about 15 minutes.

Meanwhile, warm the tortillas by placing them in a dry sauté pan over medium heat; heat them until they smell slightly toasty, with a few browned or darkened spots, 15 to 30 seconds per side. Place them in a dry kitchen towel to keep them warm.

TO SERVE: Make the tacos by spooning about 2 tablespoons of the gribenes in salsa verde to each tortilla and topping with the pickled red cabbage, fried shallots, and 1 to 2 teaspoons of the roasted tomato, arbol chile, and garlic salsa. Serve immediately.

NOTE: Fried shallots can be found at nearly any Asian supermarket.

CORN TORTILLAS

MAKES ABOUT 10 TORTILLAS

2 cups masa harina (such as Maseca)

½ teaspoon salt

1¾ cups plus 1 tablespoon warm water

1 teaspoon fish sauce

Preheat cooking surface, whether a comal or a large sauté pan, to approximately 450°F over medium heat. Combine the masa harina and salt in a large metal mixing bowl. Mix with hands to ensure even distribution of salt throughout masa.

Add 1 cup of warm water and the fish sauce to the dry masa mixture. Shape your hand like a claw and begin stirring in a clockwise motion to mix. The dough will be crumbly (similar to pie dough) at this point. Begin massaging the masa, using both hands, ensuring even distribution of water to flour, forming a dough ball. Continue adding ¼ cup of water a time (reserving the extra tablespoon until the end) and then mixing until the masa is wet to the touch but doesn't stick to your hands.

Portion the masa into walnut-sized balls, about 1½ ounces each. Keep the portioned balls beneath a damp towel to avoid moisture loss. Trim a gallon-sized food storage or freezer bag into two 8-inch squares for lining the tortilla press. With your hands, lightly flatten one masa ball (to about ¼ inch thick), then place it on the base of the tortilla press, lined with one of the plastic squares. Top with the other plastic square then firmly but gently lower the top of the press to flatten the masa ball into a thin tortilla.

Using a smooth, quick backhanded gesture, lay the tortilla on your cooking surface, ensuring that you leave no air bubbles between the tortilla and cooking surface (this will negatively impact the final product). Cook the first side until you just begin to see the tortilla curl at the edges, about 15 seconds. Cook the second side for 30-45 seconds. At 30 seconds, begin feeling the bottom of the tortilla. The tortilla should be dry to the touch. Flip the tortilla for the final cooking step, about 15 seconds, after which a properly cooked tortilla will begin to visibly puff (the top surface rising as steam is created inside).

Remove the tortilla and repeat with remaining masa balls.

This dish is, in many ways, Israel on a plate. It combines Sephardic flavors from the shawarma seasoning and tahini with a classic Ashkenazi dish, *holishkes*, in a fully integrated, updated, and contemporary way. Indeed, Jerusalem mixed grill is itself a quintessential Israeli dish and a recent one. It was created in the shadow of Jerusalem's Machane Yehuda Market no earlier than the late 1960s.

But it's the flavors, not the backstory, that make the dish. Specifically, it's the combination of the sweet, evocative warming flavors from the cardamom and the creaminess and bitter notes of the tahini (both Sephardic), on the one hand, with the savory chicken and chicken parts inside the stuffed cabbage. For those who may not be partial to the idea of offal, the shawarma seasoning makes this dish a great way to start down that path.

HOLISHKES OF JERUSALEM MIXED GRILL AND JASMINE RICE
SERVES 4 TO 6

FOR THE HOLISHKES:

Salt

1 large head green cabbage

About ½ cup Chicken Stock (page 151)

FOR THE JERUSALEM MIXED GRILL FILLING:

¼ pound ground chicken breast

¼ pound ground chicken hearts

¼ pound chicken livers, finely chopped

½ cup cooked and cooled rice (preferably jasmine)

2 tablespoons Poultry Shawarma Spice Blend (page 183)

2 tablespoons extra-virgin olive oil

FOR THE TOMATO-TAHINI SAUCE:

1 tablespoon extra-virgin olive oil

TO MAKE THE HOLISHKES: Bring a large pot of salted water to a boil over high heat. Meanwhile, remove and reserve any large, damaged outer leaves from the cabbage head (you'll use them later in the recipe). Cut out the core of the cabbage with a sharp knife and carefully pull off the rest of the leaves, keeping them whole and as undamaged as possible.

Blanch the cabbage leaves in the boiling water for 5 minutes, or until pliable. Run the leaves under cold water to cool them. Carefully cut out the hard center vein of the cabbage leaves so they will be easier to roll up. Take the reserved big outer leaves and lay them on the bottom of a glass or ceramic baking dish, letting part of the leaves hang out the sides of the pan. This insulation will prevent the cabbage rolls from burning on the bottom when baked.

Set aside 16 of the best-looking leaves to make the cabbage rolls. Not all of the leaves will be used: just the prettiest ones. Reserve the remainder of the cabbage for a different use (for example: cabbage soup, a stir-fry or lo mein dish, or a slaw).

TO MAKE THE MIXED GRILL FILLING: Preheat the oven to 350°F.

Combine the ground chicken breast, ground chicken hearts, chopped chicken liver, cooked rice, shawarma spice blend, and olive oil in a large bowl and mix well to combine. Place 2 tablespoons of

(continued)

½ cup tomato paste

1 clove garlic, minced

Salt

1 pinch nutritional yeast (optional; for additional savory character)

½ cup tahini paste

Juice of 1 lemon

1 cup water

FOR THE GARNISH:

Amba Sauce (page 165)

Tomato Powder (page 188; optional)

the filling mixture in the center of each cabbage leaf, fold the sides over the filling, and then roll them up. Transfer the rolls, seam-side down, to the bottom of a 9 × 13-inch glass or ceramic baking dish. Pour enough of the chicken stock around the baking dish to just cover the bottom. Cook the rolls until the filling is cooked through, about 20 minutes.

TO MAKE THE TOMATO-TAHINI SAUCE: While the rolls are in the oven, heat the olive oil in a small sauté pan, add the tomato paste, and fry it just long enough to draw the raw flavor out, about 15 seconds. Add the garlic and a pinch of salt to the bowl of a food processor through the feed tube and process to mince the garlic. Add the nutritional yeast (if using), tahini, tomato paste, and lemon juice to the bowl and process to combine. With the food processor running, add the water through the feed tube in a steady stream to form a smooth, creamy sauce approximately the thickness of heavy cream. You may not need all the water. Taste the sauce and adjust the balance of water, salt, and lemon juice as necessary. Turn the tahini sauce out into a bowl.

TO SERVE: Using a spatula or palate knife, spread a stripe of the tomato-tahini sauce across each plate. Top the stripe with two holishkes. Garnish with a dollop of the amba sauce in between the two holishkes and sprinkle with tomato powder (if using).

NOTE: Ask your butcher to grind the chicken hearts for you or do it yourself if you have a meat grinder (or the appropriate attachment for a standing mixer). You can also achieve excellent results mincing with a sharp chef's knife.

srael is, without a doubt, the world's greatest research and development laboratory for kosher cuisine. Flavors and combinations and techniques that have been initially developed elsewhere (including in the land of Palestine) crash together in a good way, creating new combinations and looking at old ones in new ways.

One place that has experienced quite a bit of that focus is the central pocket of pita. There are the Israeli street food classics—falafel and shawarma—of course. Absolutely. Maybe none better. At Miznon restaurant in Tel Aviv (now also in Paris, Vienna, Melbourne, and New York), those classics are nothing more than a theme upon which to work variations. Miznon is all about gourmet food done as street food all packed in a pita.

And that is the inspiration for this dish. My take on the theme employs a flavor combination that is one of my favorite new-classic affinities: coffee and lamb. It may seem counterintuitive at first blush, but the acidity, hints of sweetness, and slight bitterness in coffee pairs well with the richness and hint of pungency in lamb (albeit the pronounced bitterness of dark roasts can overwhelm the dish).

COFFEE BRAISED LAMB SHOULDER IN PITA

SERVES 4 TO 6

2 pounds boneless lamb shoulder, cut into 1-inch cubes

Salt and freshly ground black pepper

3 tablespoons extra-virgin olive oil

1 large onion, diced

1 medium carrot, diced

1 bulb fennel, cored and diced (fronds and stalks reserved for another purpose)

4 cloves garlic, minced

2 sprigs rosemary

2 sprigs thyme

4 cups brewed coffee (preferably not a dark roast)

1 cup Beef Stock (page 152)

4 to 6 pita rounds

Tahini Sauce (page 159)

Pickled Red Cabbage (page 177)

Season the lamb with salt and pepper.

Heat the olive oil in a Dutch oven over high heat. When the oil shimmers (but before it smokes), add the lamb to the pot, working in batches, and sear on all sides until browned. Remove the lamb to a bowl and reduce the heat to low. Add the onion, carrot, and fennel to the pot and sweat for 2 to 3 minutes, scraping the bottom of the pan with a wooden spoon and using the liquid released by the aromatic vegetables to deglaze the pan. Return the lamb to the pot, add the garlic, rosemary, and thyme, and pour the coffee and beef stock over the lamb to cover. Bring to a boil, then reduce the heat to low and cover. Maintain a simmer and cook until the lamb is tender, about 2 hours. Remove the lamb from the pot using a slotted spoon and set aside to cool. Once the lamb is cool enough to handle, shred it using two forks (or your hands).

Meanwhile, reduce the remaining braising liquid until it coats the back of a spoon. Taste the sauce for seasoning and adjust accordingly.

Cut the pitas in half. Drizzle some tahini sauce into the base of each pita pocket. Top with the shredded lamb, tahini sauce, pickled cabbage, and some more sauce.

t's hard to find a place in Israel without a shawarma stand nearby. That's one of Israel's charms. As long as there's a shawarma stand there's good food. Shawarma, at these places, is made from marinated meat slow-roasted on a vertical spit for many hours. While the meat can be anything from lamb or beef to chicken (or combinations of anything in that range), in Israel it's often turkey. The meat is carved off the spit in thin, wide strips and stuffed inside a flatbread along with a variety of pickles and vegetables and with various sauces.

Unless you've got a vertical spit hanging around, homemade shawarma has to be different. Here, I slow roast the turkey breast and serve it along with my versions of classic shawarma accompaniments. The garlic and herbs give the tahini another dimension.

TURKEY SHAWARMA WITH GARLIC AND HERB TAHINI AND PICKLED RED CABBAGE

SERVES 4

FOR THE TURKEY:

2 pounds boneless, skinless turkey breasts (or 2 single 1-pound breasts)

2 tablespoons fresh lemon juice

¼ cup extra-virgin olive oil

¼ cup Poultry Shawarma Spice Blend (page 183)

1 tablespoon grapeseed, canola, or another neutral oil

FOR THE GARLIC AND HERB TAHINI SAUCE:

4 cloves garlic, crushed

¼ cup minced fresh parsley

¼ cup minced fresh basil (or, better yet, lemon basil)

1 teaspoon salt (plus more if necessary)

1 cup tahini paste

¼ cup fresh lemon juice (plus more if necessary)

1 cup water

1 tablespoon ground sumac (for garnish for its wonderfully tart and fruity flavor and deep color)

FOR SERVING:

Pickled Red Cabbage (page 177)

4 to 8 whole pita breads, cut in half

TO MAKE THE TURKEY: Preheat the oven to 300°F. Place the turkey breasts in a large bowl. Whisk together the lemon juice, olive oil, and shawarma spice blend until thoroughly combined. Massage the turkey breasts with the lemon juice–spice mixture. Ideally, vacuum seal the turkey and marinate in a sous vide bag or, failing that, place the marinated meat in a zip-top bag. Refrigerate for at least 4 hours, preferably overnight.

Remove the turkey breasts from the marinade and wipe off any excess marinade. Heat the grapeseed or canola oil in an oven-safe sauté pan (large enough to fit both turkey breasts) over high heat. Sear the turkey breasts on each side just until they're browned. Transfer the pan to the oven and roast for 45 minutes to 1 hour, until the internal temperature in the thickest part of the breast reaches 165°F on an instant-read or meat thermometer. Remove the turkey from the pan and let rest on a cutting board for 10 minutes before cutting into thin slices against the grain.

TO MAKE THE GARLIC AND HERB TAHINI SAUCE: While the turkey breasts roast, combine the garlic, parsley, basil, and salt in the bowl of a food processor and process to thoroughly combine. Add the tahini and lemon juice and purée. Add ¾ cup water through the feed tube in a steady stream to form a smooth, creamy sauce approximately the thickness of heavy cream. Taste the sauce and adjust the balance of salt and lemon juice as necessary. If the sauce is too thick, add additional water. The exact amounts of water, lemon juice, and salt will depend on the exact properties of the tahini paste. Turn the tahini sauce out into a bowl and garnish with the sumac.

TO SERVE: Arrange the sliced turkey attractively on one side of a serving plate along with a pile of pickled red cabbage, little bowls of the garlic-herb tahini sauce, and the half pita rounds for diners to build their own shawarma sandwiches.

irria, originally from the Mexican state of Jalisco (think Guadalajara and Puerto Vallarta) is meat braised slowly in a broth spiked with cinnamon, cloves, and vinegar, yielding a thick, rich, and utterly exhilarating stew. Birria can be made with just about any red meat. Goat is the most classic meat for birria in Jalisco, but beef is also common, especially in Mexico's north.

While goat may be a bit challenging for the American palate, lamb is less so and is an excellent—and readily available—substitute with a similar flavor profile. Personally, I love the way the gaminess of lamb pairs with the sweet spices and acidity of the birria broth. Here, instead of serving the dish in a broth, I braise the lamb shanks to the point of tenderness and use the classic birria flavors for the sauce.

A Mexican-style comal is a useful tool for preparing the tortillas for tacos. In addition to tortillas, this smooth, flat griddle is regularly used to toast spices and nuts as well as searing meat. A heavy sauté pan or cast-iron skillet makes a fine substitute.

LAMB SHANK "BIRRIA"

SERVES 4

FOR THE "BIRRIA":
5 dried guajillo chiles
2 dried pasilla chiles
¼ cup red wine vinegar
1 tablespoon grapeseed, canola, or another neutral oil
1 medium white onion, chopped
1 bulb fennel, cored and chopped (fronds and stalks reserved for another purpose)
1 medium carrot, chopped
Salt
1 stick canela (or cinnamon), crushed
6 whole cloves
4 allspice berries
½ teaspoon minced fresh ginger
4 lamb shanks (¾ to 1 pound each)
Freshly ground black pepper
6 cups Beef Stock (page 152)
1 tablespoon light soy sauce (optional)
1 shallot, minced

Preheat a large sauté pan over medium heat.

Cut the stems off the guajillo and pasilla chiles, removing the seeds as you do so. Toast the chiles in the pan until they just begin to develop toasted dark marks, about 30 seconds. Flip the chiles and toast the other side. Soak the chiles in a bowl of hot water for 30 minutes, or until they are tender and pliable. Remove them from the water and place in the bowl of a high-speed blender or food processor, add the vinegar, and process to a smooth paste, about 30 seconds, scraping the sides of the bowl occasionally, as needed.

Combine the oil, onion, fennel, and carrot in a large heavy pot. Place over low heat and season with salt. Cover and sweat the aromatics for 5 minutes.

Meanwhile, in a spice grinder, grind the canela, cloves, allspice, and ginger to a powder. Season the lamb shanks with salt and pepper and add them to the pot. Strain the ground spices through a fine-mesh strainer and sprinkle them over the shanks. Cover the shanks with beef stock, soy sauce (if using), and chile-vinegar paste, and turn the heat up to high. Bring to a boil, then immediately reduce the heat to maintain a simmer. Cover and braise for 3 hours, or until the meat is falling off the bone, periodically flipping the shanks.

(continued)

At least 8 corn tortillas (page 77)

½ head green cabbage, cored and shredded

1 bunch cilantro, stemmed and chopped

4 to 8 árbol chiles

Combine the shallots and 2 cups of the birria braising liquid in a small saucepan. Bring to a boil over medium-high heat, lower the heat to maintain a simmer, and reduce by half, about 20-30 minutes.

Meanwhile, heat a comal or large heavy skillet over high heat. Using tongs, place two or three tortillas on the pan for a few seconds, until they soften and just start to mark. Flip the tortillas and do the same on the other side. Place the tortillas in a tortilla warmer or wrap in a clean dish towel and repeat for the remaining tortillas.

Using tongs, place a lamb shank in each of four wide bowls and ladle the braising liquid sauce over the meat. Garnish with the cabbage, cilantro, and árbol chiles and serve with the warmed tortillas.

NOTE: For a more formal presentation, swipe the birria sauce diagonally on the plate, as if dressing a bagel. Neatly pile a small amount of the shredded cabbage on top of the sauce then top with a lamb shank. Lightly brush or drizzle the shank with more of the sauce and serve.

Goulash was the dish of Hungarian Jews—of which my paternal grandfather was one—as it was of pretty much all Hungarians. While this classic peasant dish was not limited to beef as it hit American shores, it pretty much became a beef dish, primarily if not exclusively.

Especially in view of the fact that beef was not always the meat in goulash, no particular cut of beef is obligatory. Short ribs are one of my favorites for goulash. Their rich flavor pairs well with the paprika and they benefit from the long, slow cook. Definitely do not skimp on the paprika, either in quantity or quality. This isn't the dish for the smoked stuff or the spicy stuff. Use good-quality Hungarian sweet paprika.

SHORT RIB GOULASH

SERVES 4

2 pounds beef short ribs

Salt and freshly ground black pepper

2 tablespoons grapeseed, canola, or another neutral oil

1 large onion, diced

2 large leeks, white parts only, cleaned, halved lengthwise, and thinly sliced across

1 medium carrot, diced

1 bulb fennel, cored and diced (fronds and stalks reserved for another purpose)

4 cloves garlic, minced

1 tablespoon fresh thyme leaves

¼ cup sweet Hungarian paprika

1 cup red wine

2 cups Beef Stock (page 152)

1 pound egg noodles

FOR THE GARNISH:

Herb Oil (page 191)

Season the short ribs with salt and pepper.

Heat the oil in a Dutch oven over medium heat. When the oil shimmers (but before it smokes), add the short ribs to the pot and sear on all sides until browned, about 8 minutes total. Remove the short ribs from the pot and turn the heat down to low. Add the onion, leeks, carrots, and fennel to the pot, season with salt, and sweat for 2 to 3 minutes. Add the garlic and thyme and continue to sweat for 2 to 3 more minutes, until the vegetables begin to give up the ghost and release their juices.

Sprinkle the paprika over the vegetables and, using a wooden spoon or plastic spatula, stir to integrate the spice thoroughly into the vegetables. Return the short ribs to the pot and stir again to combine with the vegetables and the paprika. Turn the heat up to high and add the red wine and beef stock. When the liquid comes to a boil, turn the heat down to low and braise, covered, until the meat is falling off the bone, about 2 hours.

About 1 hour 45 minutes into the braise, bring another pot of salted water to a boil. Add the egg noodles and cook until they are al dente in texture, about 10 minutes, or according to the package instructions. Drain the noodles.

TO SERVE: Arrange some egg noodles on one side of a shallow bowl. Ladle the goulash from the other side of the bowl and lapping up on the noodles. Garnish around the edge of the bowl opposite the noodles with the herb oil. Repeat for the remaining servings.

GLOBAL RECIPES

FOR THE MODERN KOSHER TABLE

Jews have always eaten dishes that weren't ethnically Jewish. As the Jewish people traveled throughout the world in the years, decades, centuries, and ultimately millennia following the fall of the Second Temple in Jerusalem, they carried with them their dietary laws. Forced to adapt the application of those laws to the meats and vegetables—and the cuisines—of their new countries, they both created new dishes and adapted those of their hosts.

Several challenges, each of which offer significant opportunities, present themselves in the process of adapting classic recipes from non-ethnically Jewish cuisines to the Jewish table. First, there are some foods that are, plainly and simply, *treif* (Yiddish: טרייף or *treyf*, derived from Hebrew טְרֵפָה *trēfáh*), forbidden by the laws of kashrut. There's no work-around for a classic crab dish other than not using the shellfish. That's the approach for the California Fisherman's Cioppino (page 125). Without shellfish there's no inherent reason the dish isn't kosher (and it does hark back to the origin of the dish).

Conversely, there's nothing inherently treif about butter. But because the laws of kashrut essentially forbid the use of a dairy product and meat in the same meal, butter cannot be used in the sauce for Veal Piccata (page 137). But schmaltz (rendered chicken fat; recipe on page 187) as a substitute would be both kosher and delicious.

Similarly, while a classic dish like beef tartare is an excellent and otherwise kosher starter, the prohibition of dairy and meat in the same meal means that it can't be served as a starter if the main course is going to be Lasagnette of Mushrooms, House-made Ricotta, and Mint-Pepita Pesto (page 123) or another dish including dairy. But what about Beet Tartare with Greek Yogurt, Capers, and Fenugreek Salt (page 92)? By swapping the beef out for beet (it's just *one letter*), the entire meal becomes kosher.

SMALL
PLATES

*A*rancini is Italian for "no-waste." At the most basic level, they're fried stuffed rice balls filled most commonly with a meat ragu, peas, or cheese. Perhaps most commonly, however, they're a vehicle for the use of last night's risotto dish.

I would never want to see an ounce of my Risotto of Mushrooms and Peas (page 117) go to waste. So, with that in mind, here's a recipe to make sure that it does not. The key to the dish is the refrigeration of the arancini balls to let them set before frying. If you have just made your risotto, take the time to fully chill it in the refrigerator until it is firm to the touch. Do not skimp on the time for that step.

ARANCINI OF MOZZARELLA AND MUSHROOM RISOTTO

SERVES 4

2 cups Risotto of Mushrooms and Peas (page 117)

2 large eggs, beaten

½ cup grated Parmesan cheese

1½ cups Italian-style bread crumbs

2 ounces fresh mozzarella cheese, cut into ½-inch cubes

Grapeseed, canola, or another neutral oil, for frying

Salt

Quick Tomato Sauce (page 173) or Tomato Confit (page 193).

It is crucial to start with fully cooled risotto. Once it is, combine the eggs, risotto, Parmesan, and ½ cup of the bread crumbs in a large bowl to combine. Place the remaining breadcrumbs in a medium bowl. Using your hands, form the mixture into four balls (2 to 3 tablespoons of risotto each), continuing to roll them in your palm until they form a sphere. Insert your finger into the center of each ball, insert a mozzarella cube in the hole, and close the hole by re-forming the sphere around it. Repeat with the remaining balls. Roll the balls in the remaining bread crumbs and, crucially, place them in the refrigerator to chill and set, at least 1 hour.

Pour the oil into a heavy medium pot or Dutch oven fitted with a candy or frying thermometer to a depth of 2 inches. Heat over medium heat until the thermometer reads 350°F. Carefully lower the rice balls into the oil (working in batches depending on the size of your pot) using a slotted spoon or spider and fry until deep golden brown, 6 to 8 minutes. Transfer the rice balls to paper towels to drain and season with salt. Serve over tomato sauce or tomato confit.

t one level this dish is playing on the color and the "meatiness" of beets and using them in a dish inspired by the classic French beef tartare. This version of beet tartare is decidedly Mediterranean in tone—it's the type of thing you might see on the menu at a high-end Tel Aviv restaurant—featuring a bevy of complementary Mediterranean ingredients and flavors stepping forward. The capers of the original fit the theme, but Greek-style yogurt, fenugreek salt, and fresh rosemary flowers complete the picture. The sweet, nutty, and ever-so-slightly bitter flavor of the fenugreek married with the salt does some crucial heavy lifting.

If you wanted to take it in a Mexican direction, use chopped olives instead of capers, swap out the Greek yogurt for Mexican crema, and dust the plate with oregano instead of the fenugreek salt. Would you rather go Scandinavian? Sour cream instead of yogurt together with ground dill (the capers work fine).

BEET TARTARE WITH GREEK YOGURT, CAPERS, AND FENUGREEK SALT

SERVES 4

FOR THE BEET TARTARE:

1 pound (about 4) medium beets, scrubbed

2 tablespoons extra-virgin olive oil (plus more to coat the beets)

1 medium shallot, minced

3 tablespoons capers in brine, rinsed

Salt and freshly ground black pepper

2 tablespoons balsamic vinegar reduction (see Note)

2 tablespoons lime zest

FOR THE FENUGREEK SALT:

3 tablespoons dried fenugreek leaves (see Note)

½ teaspoon salt (plus more as needed)

FOR THE GARNISH:

1 cup plain Greek-style yogurt

¼ cup dried oregano

12 rosemary (or other herb) flowers (optional)

TO MAKE THE BEET TARTARE: Preheat the oven to 375°F.

Coat the beets lightly with oil, wrap them in aluminum foil, and place them on a baking sheet. Roast in the oven until they can be easily pierced through with a knife, 45 to 60 minutes. Remove the beets from the oven, unwrap them, allow to cool to room temperature, and then place them in the refrigerator to chill. When they are cold enough to handle, peel the beets with your hands. With a little effort, the skins should slip right off.

Slice the beets into ⅛-inch segments and then into ⅛-inch dice. Add the olive oil, shallot, capers, salt and pepper to taste, the balsamic vinegar glaze, and lime zest and fold to combine thoroughly.

TO MAKE THE FENUGREEK SALT: Put the fenugreek leaves and salt in a spice grinder and grind to a powder. Taste the powder; add more salt and re-grind as necessary.

TO SERVE: Dust a plate with the fenugreek salt. Using a ring mold (or, failing that, a biscuit cutter, circle cookie cutter, or even a tuna can with both top and bottom removed), place the tartare on a plate in a neat cylinder and press with the base of a wine glass or wooden spoon to compact. Spoon a dollop of the yogurt on top. Carefully lift off the ring mold. Garnish the tartare with oregano and rosemary flowers and plate by sprinkling with the fenugreek salt using a shaker (or through a fine sieve). Repeat to make four plates.

NOTE: Dried fenugreek leaves are readily available at most Middle Eastern and Indian markets. They are not the same as the fenugreek seeds or the powder made from them, though both are delicious and have many uses in the kitchen. For the balsamic vinegar reduction, you can either use a bottled balsamic glaze or make it as in the first step of the Spiced Red and Golden Beet Tzimmes (page 39), omitting the Tajin spice blend.

There's something about the original Caesar salad. Perhaps it's the elegant perfection of a few good ingredients combined in just the right proportions. And there's something about the crisp freshness and slight bitterness of the romaine lettuce, the soothing umami of the Parmesan cheese, the textural contrast of the big, garlicky crouton, and the way the acidity, richness, and mysteriously funky flavors of the dressing manage to achieve simplicity and depth at the same time. It all just fits together gracefully.

As good as that original salad—invented by Caesar Cardini at his Tijuana restaurant (or, perhaps, invented by his chef, Livio Santini, depending on whose story is to be believed) and still served there today—truly is, it may be a bit of a hard ask for the average home cook. How many kitchens come with two-foot wooden bowls, and how many home cooks can "whisk" a dressing using a wooden paddle?

This version is a bit more friendly to the average home kitchen and its chef. I've never known anyone bothered by leftover croutons; besides keeping well and making a great snack, they pulverize into delicious bread crumbs.

"ORIGINAL" CAESAR'S RESTAURANTE BAR CAESAR SALAD

SERVES 4

FOR THE CROUTONS:

1 clove garlic

2 tablespoons extra-virgin olive oil

2 tablespoons butter

1 small French baguette (about 9 ounces)

2 tablespoons grated Parmesan cheese

Paprika for garnish

FOR THE SALAD:

20 romaine lettuce leaves

1 teaspoon Worcestershire sauce

1 tablespoon Dijon mustard

6 anchovy fillets, rinsed

1 clove garlic, crushed

Juice of 2 limes

½ cup grated or finely shredded Parmesan cheese

2 large egg yolks

¾ cup extra-virgin olive oil

Freshly ground black pepper

TO MAKE THE CROUTONS: Lightly crush the garlic and put it in a ramekin or small bowl, add the olive oil, and leave to infuse overnight.

Preheat oven to 350°F and line a baking sheet with parchment paper.

Remove garlic slices from oil. In a large skillet, melt the butter over low heat. Turn off the heat and add the garlic oil. Cut the baguette into thick slices and coat each with garlic butter. Arrange the baguette slices on the prepared baking sheet and sprinkle each with the cheese and paprika. Bake until just crisp, 8 to 10 minutes. The croutons can be made ahead and stored in an airtight container unrefrigerated for up to 2 weeks.

TO MAKE THE SALAD: Clean the lettuce leaves thoroughly and refrigerate until crisp, at least 1 hour.

In a food processor, combine the Worcestershire sauce, mustard, anchovies, garlic, lime juice, and ¼ cup of the cheese and process to form a paste. Add the egg yolks and process to blend thoroughly. Then, with the food processor still running, slowly add the olive oil

(continued)

in a thin stream until the dressing ingredients are thoroughly combined; in other words, the dressing is emulsified.

Pour half of the dressing into a salad bowl, then add whole romaine lettuce leaves and gently roll them until they are coated with the dressing. If more dressing is needed, add some and continue gently rolling the leaves. Any unused dressing can keep in the refrigerator, properly sealed, for up to 1 week. Divide the dressed leaves among four salad plates and top with the remaining ¼ cup cheese and one large crouton per plate (you could add a second, but any unused croutons make for great bread crumbs). Grind some pepper on top.

NOTE: For an extra flourish of "cheffy" elegance (and drama), serve the salad for all diners on an attractive cutting board (or marble pastry slab), pouring the dressing across the board first, then attractively arranging the romaine leaves and croutons on top of the dressing before raining the finishing Parmesan over it all.

arlic soup is a Spanish classic. But, like so many other great dishes of that country, it relies on a pork product—*jamon serrano* in this case—for an important jolt of umami flavor. But a similar and equally delicious effect can be achieved by swapping out the ham for oven-dried tomatoes because the drying process intensifies and concentrates the inherent sweet, salty, and umami flavors of the tomatoes.

One ingredient that is critical to this recipe is the Oloroso sherry. I specifically call for Oloroso sherry, which is on the drier end of the sherry spectrum but with heavier body, darker color, and just a hint of sweetness to go with its walnut and caramel flavors.

SPANISH GARLIC SOUP WITH OVEN-DRIED TOMATOES AND SOURDOUGH CROUTONS

SERVES 4

FOR THE CROUTONS:

1 sourdough or French baguette (about 9 ounces)

¼ cup extra-virgin olive oil

Spanish sweet paprika for garnish

FOR THE SOUP:

¼ cup extra-virgin olive oil

10 cloves garlic, peeled

1 tablespoon Spanish sweet paprika

6 cups Roast Vegetable Stock (page 154) or Chicken Stock (page 151)

¼ cup Oloroso sherry

4 large eggs

¼ pound Oven-Dried Tomatoes (page 188), sliced into small strips

Salt

TO MAKE THE CROUTONS: Preheat the oven to 350°F.

Cut the baguette into thick slices and brush both sides of each slice with the olive oil. Line a baking sheet with parchment paper. Arrange the baguette slices on the baking sheet and sprinkle each with paprika. Bake until just crisp, 8 to 10 minutes. You can make the croutons ahead and store in airtight containers at room temperature for up to 3 days or in the freezer for up to 2 weeks.

TO MAKE THE SOUP: Heat the olive oil in a large soup pot over medium heat and gently cook the garlic until it is softened but not browned, about 4 minutes. Transfer the softened garlic to a bowl and lightly crush with a fork. Add the paprika to the oil in the pot, then stir in the stock and sherry. Return the pot to the stovetop and bring to a boil over medium-high heat. Reduce the heat to maintain a simmer and stir the crushed garlic back into the pot. Cook, stirring occasionally, until the flavors meld, about 15 minutes.

With the soup simmering, break the eggs one at a time into a small bowl and tip each egg into the soup, swirling gently around each egg with a wooden spoon. Poach each egg for about 4 minutes, until the whites firm and seal the yolk inside.

Ladle into serving bowls. Divide the poached eggs among them and top each with a few of the oven-dried tomato strips. Add a crouton to each bowl. Pass the remaining croutons.

Much of Sephardic cuisine began its life as Islamic (Moorish) dishes filtered through the laws of kosher. One such dish is gazpacho, that familiar cold tomato soup that is so perfect for hot evenings at the height of summer. The name itself gives clues—albeit potentially conflicting ones—as to the origin of the dish. The most frequently cited source for the origin of the word *gazpacho* is the Mozarab word *caspa*, meaning "fragments" or "residue," possibly alluding to the bits of chopped vegetables and small chunks of bread in the soup. Others, including food writer José Briz (author of *Libro del gazpacho y de los gazpachos*), assert it comes from the Hebrew word *gazaz* (גזז), meaning "shear" or "break into pieces."

We almost indelibly associate gazpacho with tomatoes, though the dish was originally made without them. Gazpacho is surely pre-Columbian in origin and may well be of Roman descent. At its core gazpacho incorporates bits of bread (often stale bread soaked in water) and olive oil, and sometimes garlic and vinegar. Indeed, in Spain today there are many varieties of gazpacho that do not include tomatoes. White gazpacho based on garlic and almonds is common, as are pepper-based versions and more.

While two millennia of gazpacho history and tradition are both interesting and important, in making this dish I'm more interested in what gazpacho has become than where it originated. My focus in creating this version of gazpacho was zeroing in on what modern gazpacho is all about: how the freshest of ingredients crash against each other, melding into a new and different flavor that is entirely its own thing.

GAZPACHO WITH CROUTONS AND CILANTRO OIL
SERVES 4 TO 6

1 Persian cucumber

2 large red bell peppers

1½ pounds (about 4 medium) incredibly, supremely flavorful tomatoes

½ teaspoon salt (plus more as needed)

¼ cup sherry vinegar (plus more as needed)

2 to 3 tablespoons extra-virgin olive oil (plus more as needed)

Croutons (page 197)

Cilantro Oil (page 191)

Attractive cilantro leaves

Roughly chop the vegetables. Put the chopped cucumber in the work bowl of a high-speed blender or food processor. Starting on the lowest setting possible (or by pulsing), begin puréeing the cucumber, gradually raising the speed until the cucumber is completely liquefied. Return the processor to its lowest setting. Add the bell pepper to the work bowl and repeat the previous step with the pepper. Do the same with the tomatoes, one at a time. Add the salt, vinegar, and olive oil and taste the soup; adjust the salt, pepper, and vinegar balance as needed. Refrigerate for at least 30 minutes up to an hour.

Strain the purée through a fine-mesh sieve or strainer. Indeed, do so more than once until you achieve a perfectly smooth and silky texture. Pour the soup into bowls and arrange some of the croutons around the rim of each bowl. Garnish with a bit of cilantro oil and cilantro leaves in the middle of the bowl.

Vichyssoise, the familiar cold leek and potato soup, is widely assumed to be a classic French dish. In fact, it was created in 1910 by Chef Louis Diat at New York's Ritz-Carlton Hotel. What the dish was, in reality, was a cold, puréed version of the *parmentier*, a truly classic French potato and leek soup.

For this take on the dish, continuing in Diat's footsteps, I retained the Vichyssoise's silky smooth, puréed texture and swapped in Jerusalem artichokes (a.k.a. sunchokes) for some of the potatoes. I also serve the soup around a flavorful island of peas and soy chorizo.

I'm not ordinarily a fan of vegan meat substitutes, but I see soy chorizo differently because it is plainly a delicious product in its own right. The way the smoky, slightly sweet and spicy flavors of the soy chorizo play here with the nutty, earthy flavors of the Jerusalem artichoke shows the value of giving the product a bit of a star turn.

While I usually make this dish with chicken stock, to serve it with a dairy meal—or to be fully vegan—use vegetable stock.

JERUSALEM ARTICHOKE "PARMENTIER" WITH PEAS AND SOY CHORIZO
SERVES 6 TO 8

FOR THE SOUP:

2 large leeks, white parts only, cleaned, halved lengthwise, and thinly sliced across

1 large white onion, diced

1 bulb fennel, cored and diced (fronds and stalks reserved for another purpose)

1 tablespoon extra-virgin olive oil

Salt

8 cups Chicken Stock (page 151) or Vegetable Stock (page 154)

½ pound (about 1 large) russet potato, roughly chopped

1½ pounds Jerusalem artichokes, peeled

FOR THE SOY CHORIZO AND PEAS:

1 small red onion, quartered and thinly sliced across

2 teaspoons extra-virgin olive oil

1 link soy chorizo, casing removed and crumbled

6 ounces frozen sweet peas, thawed

TO MAKE THE SOUP: Combine the leeks, onion, fennel, and olive oil in a soup pot, season with salt, and sweat over low heat until they give up their water and are translucent, about 3 minutes. Add the stock, increase the heat, and bring to a boil. Add the potatoes and Jerusalem artichokes and bring back to a boil. Reduce the heat to maintain a simmer and cook until the potatoes and Jerusalem artichokes lose their texture, about 30 minutes.

In a high-speed blender, purée the soup (working in batches). Strain the soup as you finish each batch. Taste the finished soup and adjust the seasonings.

TO MAKE THE SOY CHORIZO AND PEAS: Sweat the onion in the olive oil in a large sauté pan over low heat until it begins to lose its color, about 2 minutes. Turn the heat up to high, add the soy chorizo, and cook until it just begins to slightly brown, about 5 minutes. Add the peas and continue cooking until all the peas are heated through, about 3 minutes.

FOR THE GARNISH:

Pea sprouts or pea greens (optional)

TO SERVE: Place 1 to 2 tablespoons of the chorizo-pea mixture in the center of a soup bowl. Transfer the soup to a pouring vessel. A large (4-cup) measuring cup will work well. Alternatively, use a ladle. Either way, pour the soup around the chorizo-pea mixture until only the top of it is sticking above the level of the soup. Garnish with pea sprouts or greens (if using). Repeat for the remaining servings.

've professed my love for Spanish tapas, especially the Basque *pintxos* as seen in the wonderful tapas bars of old San Sebastian. Piquillo peppers stuffed with *bacalao* (salt cod) are common throughout Spain, but at La Cuchara San Telmo they swap out the peppers in favor of tomatoes and salt cod for tuna mousse.

For my version, I also use fresh dill as the herb in my vinaigrette (a play on the classic Scandinavian pairing of dill with fish), which really emphasizes the freshness of the dish. This contrasts nicely with the savory, rich stuffing and the barely cooked tomato.

TUNA-STUFFED TOMATOES WITH FRESH DILL VINAIGRETTE

SERVES 4

FOR THE STUFFED TOMATOES:

4 medium tomatoes

2 (6-ounce) cans good-quality oil-packed tuna

3 tablespoons Mayonnaise (page 168)

1 tablespoon tomato paste

1 tablespoon minced fresh parsley

FOR THE FRESH DILL VINAIGRETTE:

1 bunch fresh dill, chopped

2 shallots, chopped

½ cup Lemon and Red Wine Vinaigrette (page 175)

FOR THE GARNISH:

Spanish sweet paprika

¼ cup Amba Sauce (page 165)

Finishing salt

Radish sprouts

TO MAKE THE TOMATOES: Bring a medium pot of water to a boil over high heat and prepare an ice bath. Skin the tomatoes by making a small (⅛ inch) X-shaped incision on the very blossom end of each tomato (opposite the stem). Add the tomatoes (two at a time if necessary) to the pot and blanch for 10 seconds, then remove and plunge into the ice bath to stop the cooking. Do not discard the boiling water because you'll need it later in this recipe; just turn the heat down and cover to maintain a simmer. When the tomatoes are cooled, peel them by pinching a bit of their skin at the incision point and gently pulling it back and down, peeling it away from the flesh of the tomato. Slice the tops off and, using a teaspoon or paring knife, remove the seeds and insides. Refresh the ice in the ice bath.

Put the tuna, mayonnaise, tomato paste, and parsley in the bowl of a food processor and pulse to combine, scraping the sides of the bowl occasionally as needed, then process to a smooth, mousse-like texture, about 2 minutes. Stuff the tomatoes with the mousse, firmly pressing the filling down. Set aside until the vinaigrette is made. You can make the recipe up to this point up to 1 hour ahead; brush the stuffed tomatoes with olive oil to prevent them from drying out, cover with plastic wrap, and transfer to the refrigerator.

TO MAKE THE FRESH DILL VINAIGRETTE: Bring the water back to a boil and blanch the fresh dill in the water to set the bright, green color, about 10 seconds. Plunge the dill into the ice bath to stop the cooking, then remove and wring dry. Combine the dill, shallots, and lemon and red wine vinaigrette in the bowl of a high-speed blender or food processor. Starting on the lowest speed, blend the vinaigrette to combine, gradually increasing the speed until it achieves a tight, puréed sauce texture, about 1 minute.

TO SERVE: Place a stuffed tomato on each plate, cut-side down. Drizzle some of the vinaigrette over the top of each tomato. Garnish with sprinkles of paprika, 1 tablespoon of the amba sauce, some crystals of finishing salt, and radish sprouts, and serve.

*R*illettes are a classic French dish—originally, like confit, a preservation technique—of chopped, salted pork meat slow-cooked in fat, shredded, and cooled to form a paste. At their core, though, rilletes are just another way of marrying protein and fat into a flavor bomb. Pork, of course, is not kosher, but the basic concept of rilletes isn't inherently limited to pork. As chefs like Thomas Keller and Eric Ripert have shown, salmon, a fatty protein like pork, works equally well for rilletes.

This take on the original (and on Keller's and Ripert's versions) also has the benefit of being incredibly easy. The toughest part may be gently mixing all the ingredients to fully combine them without overmixing and making something of a purée. The key to this, as in so many recipes, is a gentle hand and patience.

SALMON RILLETTES WITH SOURDOUGH TOAST POINTS

MAKES APPROXIMATELY 20 HORS D'OEUVRE PORTIONS

FOR THE TOAST POINTS:

10 slices sourdough bread

3 tablespoons butter, melted

¼ teaspoon salt

FOR THE SALMON RILLETTES:

2 scallions

2 cups dry white wine (such as sauvignon blanc)

1 pound skinless salmon fillets, cut into 1-inch pieces

3 ounces smoked salmon, cut into ¼-inch pieces

½ cup Mayonnaise (page 168) (plus more as needed)

1 tablespoon fresh lemon juice (plus more as needed)

Fine sea salt and freshly ground white pepper

FOR THE GARNISH:

Capers in brine, drained

Pink Pickled Onions (page 177)

TO MAKE THE TOAST POINTS: Preheat the oven to 400°F. Cut the sourdough slices into a square shape and then cut each square diagonally to create triangles. In a small bowl, stir together the melted butter and salt. Lightly brush one side of the bread with the salted butter. Place, buttered-side up, on a baking sheet and bake for 6 to 8 minutes, until toasted. Cool on a wire rack for 30 minutes.

TO MAKE THE SALMON RILLETTES: Divide the white and green parts from the scallions. Set the greens aside, then chop the whites (you should get about 2 tablespoons) and add them to a medium saucepan along with the wine. Set over high heat and bring to a boil, then reduce the heat to low, add the salmon fillets, and cover. Poach the salmon just until opaque in the center, about 5 minutes. Carefully transfer the salmon to a paper towel–lined plate to drain. Strain the poaching liquid through a fine-mesh sieve and discard the liquid. Transfer the poached salmon to a bowl, cover, and chill until completely cooled. This can be done the night before. If you choose to do so, remove the poached salmon from the refrigerator and return to room temperature before using.

Thinly slice the reserved scallion greens (you should have about 2 tablespoons) and combine with the smoked salmon in a large bowl. Add the mayonnaise, lemon juice, white pepper, and chilled poached salmon. Gently mix until just combined. Do not overwork the mixture or it will form a paste. Taste and adjust for seasoning with salt, lemon juice, or a little more mayonnaise.

TO SERVE: Top each sourdough point with 1 to 2 tablespoons of the rilletes and finish with some capers and pink pickled onions.

There have been many waves of Jewish immigration to the Indian subcontinent, and Jews are still there today. Indeed, Judaism was one of the first—if not the first—foreign religions in India, arriving two millennia ago. In some ways, India was a particularly welcoming home for Jews. While practicing Indian Jews, of course, kept kosher, that may have been less of a separator in India than elsewhere. After all, vegetarianism is prevalent among Indians, and Muslims and many Hindus (India's two largest religious groups) do not eat pork.

While most of India's Jewish population moved to Israel after its creation in 1948, there are still pockets of Jews, in particular in South India, the home of this curry. The key to this dish is the way the richness of the oil-poached tuna is cut by the acidity of the classic coriander chutney and the way the spice of the curry ties it all together.

OIL-POACHED TUNA WITH CHETTINAD CURRY AND CORIANDER CHUTNEY

SERVES 4

FOR THE TUNA:
About 2 cups extra-virgin olive oil

1 tablespoon black peppercorns

1 tablespoon fennel seeds

1 tablespoon coriander seeds

1 teaspoon fenugreek seeds

Zest from 1 lemon, in strips

1½ to 2 pounds tuna fillets (four 6- to 8-ounce fillets)

Salt

FOR THE SPICE PASTE:
1 tablespoon coriander seeds

1 teaspoon fennel seeds

1 teaspoon cumin seeds

½ teaspoon black peppercorns

4 whole cloves

1 (3-inch) cinnamon stick, crushed

1 whole star anise

7 dried árbol chiles (or other similar dried red chiles)

4 cloves garlic, peeled

1 cup canned unsweetened coconut milk

TO MAKE THE TUNA: Preheat the oven to 225°F.

Combine the oil, peppercorns, fennel seeds, coriander seeds, fenugreek seeds, and lemon zest in a medium pot and heat to 225°F. Lightly season the tuna on both sides with salt, place in a shallow baking pan, and cover with the spiced olive oil (you may not use all of the oil, or you may need a little more depending on the size of the pan). Cover tightly with foil and transfer to the oven. Poach the tuna until the fish is opaque and white rather than translucent and red and you can see a few small whitish droplets have risen to the surface of the fish, about 15 minutes. Remove the pan from the oven, transfer the tuna to a platter, and set aside at room temperature.

TO MAKE THE SPICE PASTE: Toast the coriander seeds, fennel seeds, cumin seeds, peppercorns, cloves, cinnamon stick, star anise, and chiles in a heavy, dry skillet over medium-low heat until fragrant, about 2 to 3 minutes. Let cool, then transfer to a spice grinder (remove the stems from the chiles and break them up a bit first) and grind to a powder. Add the spice mixture along with the garlic and coconut milk to a blender or food processor and process to a smooth, wet paste, about 20 seconds.

(continued)

FOR THE CHETTINAD CURRY:

1 to 2 tablespoons grapeseed, canola, or another neutral oil

10 fresh curry leaves (or 2 tablespoons dried ground curry leaves)

1 large onion, diced

1 large tomato, diced

½ teaspoon ground turmeric

¼ teaspoon cayenne pepper

½ teaspoon sugar (optional)

Salt

FOR THE ACCOMPANIMENTS:

Coriander (Cilantro) Chutney (page 164)

Red Bell Pepper Skin Curls (page 196) for garnish

TO MAKE THE CHETTINAD CURRY: Heat the grapeseed oil in a sauté pan over medium heat. When hot, add the curry leaves and cook until fragrant, about 30 seconds. Add the onion and cook for 5 to 7 minutes, until the onion starts to brown around the edges. Add the tomatoes and cook until the tomatoes have softened. Stir in the spice paste, turmeric, cayenne, and sugar (if using) and cook until the aroma mellows, another 4 to 5 minutes. Taste and adjust the seasoning by adding salt, a little sugar (if the curry is too spicy for your taste), or both. Transfer to the bowl of a high-speed blender or food processor and purée. Strain the curry through a fine-mesh sieve and keep warm for serving.

TO SERVE: Slice the tuna fillets into four equal pieces. Pour a pool of the Chettinad curry sauce on each plate, top each with an oil-poached tuna piece, and garnish with red pepper skin curls. Spoon a broad swipe of chutney across the plate.

NOTE: Properly strained, the poaching oil can be stored in the refrigerator for up to a month and reused for your next fish poaching or frying adventure.

At the core of Judaism lies the covenant between the Jews and God. The Jews' basic obligation under that covenant is the promise to obey those commandments that God revealed to them. "All that God has commanded, we will do and we will obey" (Exodus 24:7). To be specific, there are 613 such commandments.

None of those 613, however, requires that we make latkes at Hanukkah. And yet, it seems, every year that's what we do. I get it: oil is at the core of the Hanukkah story, latkes are fried in oil, and we want to tell the story on a plate. But other things are fried in oil, too; hush puppies, for example. Hush puppies are, basically, just fried balls of cornmeal batter. There are many "urban" legends about the origin of hush puppies, most of which involve some cook somewhere trying to keep dogs quiet by appeasing them with food. There is no actual evidence to support any such story, of course, but they're fun nonetheless.

As good as ordinary hush puppies are, though, inviting chicken to the party adds another dimension. And the zingy gremolata cuts perfectly through the richness of the hush puppies and the traditional Louisiana-style rémoulade (with textural interest from the addition of cornichons and capers). This recipe calls for smoked chicken and uses a smoking gun to get there. You can smoke the chicken on an outdoor smoker, on the stovetop, or buy pre-smoked chicken at many supermarkets. Frankly, simple poached (or store-bought rotisserie or even leftover roast) chicken would make wonderful hush puppies.

SMOKED CHICKEN HUSH PUPPIES WITH RÉMOULADE AND GREMOLATA

SERVES 4

FOR THE RÉMOULADE:

1 cup Mayonnaise (page 168)

2 tablespoons Dijon mustard

1 tablespoon fresh lemon juice

1 tablespoon finely chopped fresh parsley

1 tablespoon Louisiana-style hot sauce (such as Red Rooster or Texas Pete's brands)

2 teaspoons Creole mustard

2 cloves garlic, minced

2 teaspoons capers in brine, drained and roughly chopped

4 cornichons, chopped

1 teaspoon Worcestershire sauce

1 teaspoon Spanish sweet paprika

TO MAKE THE RÉMOULADE: In a small bowl, mix together the mayonnaise, mustard, lemon juice, parsley, hot sauce, mustard, garlic, capers, cornichons, Worcestershire sauce, paprika, scallion, salt, and cayenne pepper.

TO MAKE THE SMOKED CHICKEN: In a large, deep, straight-sided skillet or heavy pot, combine the carrot, celery, onion, bay leaves, thyme, beer, and salt. Bring to a boil; reduce the heat to maintain a simmer, cover, and cook for 8 minutes. Season the chicken with salt and gently lower it into the simmering liquid (the liquid should just cover the chicken). Cover and cook until the chicken is cooked through, about 10 minutes (longer for larger, thicker thighs). Using a wide slotted spatula, remove the chicken from the liquid. Let cool, then transfer to the refrigerator to chill for at least 30 minutes or as much as overnight.

(continued)

1 scallion, finely chopped (white and green parts)

¼ teaspoon salt

FOR THE SMOKED CHICKEN:

1 carrot, roughly chopped

2 ribs celery, roughly chopped

1 small onion, roughly chopped

2 bay leaves

1 sprig thyme

3 cups beer (any good lager)

1 tablespoon salt, plus more for the chicken

2 pounds boneless, skinless chicken thigh fillets

Smoker chips of choice (pecan is a good option)

FOR THE HUSH PUPPIES:

Vegetable oil

1 cup fine cornmeal

1 tablespoon sugar

2 teaspoons baking powder

1 teaspoon salt

¼ teaspoon cayenne pepper

1 large egg, lightly beaten

¼ cup beer (same lager as above)

¼ cup unsweetened coconut cream

1 cup chopped smoked chicken (see above)

¼ cup finely chopped red onion

¼ cup finely chopped scallion greens

FOR SERVING:

½ cup Gremolata (page 195)

Parsley leaves

When the chicken has cooled, shred it and place it in a large bowl. Place the smoking chips of your choice in your smoking gun and operate according to the manufacturer's instructions, covering the bowl with plastic wrap. Allow the chicken to sit in the smoke for 5 minutes.

TO MAKE THE HUSH PUPPIES: Pour oil into a Dutch oven or deep fryer to a depth of 3 inches and bring it to 350°F.

Stir together the cornmeal, sugar, baking powder, salt, and cayenne pepper in a large bowl. Add the egg, beer, and coconut cream; stir just until moistened. Let stand for 10 minutes.

Meanwhile, preheat the oven to 200°F and, in another small bowl, combine the smoked chicken, red onion, and scallions for the filling.

Working in batches, gently roll the hush puppy dough into 2-tablespoon golf ball–sized balls. Push a hole into the middle of each ball, insert 2 teaspoons of the chicken filling, and re-form the balls. Carefully lower the balls into the hot oil using a slotted spoon. Take care not to crowd the pot. Fry until golden brown and cooked through, turning with a wooden spoon for even browning, 2 to 3 minutes. Drain on a wire rack set over paper towels. Keep warm in the preheated oven while you fry the remaining batches.

TO SERVE: Plate the dish by mounding 2 tablespoons of gremolata at one edge of a plate and topping with 1 to 3 hush puppies depending on whether serving as an appetizer or a main. Spread a line of the rémoulade across the plate, above the hush puppy.

NOTE: The recipe calls for 2 pounds of chicken but only ends up using 1 cup in the hush puppies. If you're smoking a little chicken, you might as well smoke a lot. There are no shortages of use for it—in a salad, replacing the smoked fish in the knishes (page 70), and so many more.

Today there are approximately 250,000 Jews in Argentina. It is currently the sixth largest Jewish community in the world. The majority are in Buenos Aires, though there are also Jewish communities in Rosario, Córdoba, and Santa Fe. Buenos Aires has a highly active Jewish culture with synagogues, schools, kosher restaurants, and the sorts of Jewish institutions one would expect to find in hubs like New York or London—it even has the only kosher McDonald's outside of Israel.

While the country's foods are as varied as its peoples, two things come to mind immediately: pampas beef and empanadas. The latter are Argentina's take on the classic notion of serving a protein wrapped in dough for easy transport. Indeed, the word *empanada* is derived from the Spanish verb *empanar*, "to wrap in bread." Argentina's classic empanada uses their famous beef accompanied by funky ingredients such as olives and capers and sometimes raisins.

That was the model for this recipe; however, I prefer the meaty texture hand-minced beef gives. And pairing the empanada with the classic Argentinian accompaniment, *chimichurri*, was a natural. While Argentine chimichurri is chopped, not puréed, I went with the latter approach so that the sauce would cling more effectively to the empanada. The result, while not exactly a traditional empanada from the streets of Buenos Aires—kosher, slightly modernized and all—is entirely true to its soul.

EMPANADAS OF MINCED BEEF, OLIVES, AND CAPERS WITH CHIMICHURRI

MAKES APPROXIMATELY 24 EMPANADAS

FOR THE DOUGH:

3¼ cups all-purpose flour

1 teaspoon salt

1 teaspoon baking powder

½ cup (1 stick) cold, unsalted solid margarine, cut into 1 tablespoon segments

2 large eggs, at room temperature

½ cup soy (or almond) milk

1 tablespoon distilled white vinegar

1 egg, gently beaten with a fork (for the egg wash)

FOR THE FILLING:

2 to 3 tablespoons extra-virgin olive oil

½ pound top sirloin beef, finely chopped by hand until minced (ground beef will do in a pinch)

TO MAKE THE DOUGH: Sift the flour, salt, and baking powder into the bowl of a food processor. Add the margarine, eggs, soy milk, and vinegar and pulse until the mixture resembles coarse crumbs, six or seven times. Flour your hands and work the mixture on a lightly floured surface until it becomes a well-combined dough, about another minute. Shape the dough into a ball, wrap it in plastic wrap, and refrigerate for 30 minutes to 1 hour.

MAKE THE FILLING: While the dough is resting, heat 2 tablespoons of the olive oil in a medium sauté pan over high heat. When the oil is hot, add the beef and brown on all sides, about 2 minutes. Transfer to a medium bowl. Keep the fat in the pan and, if necessary, add another tablespoon of oil. Once hot, add the onion and cook until it softens but does not brown, about 5 minutes. Add the tomatoes and cook down for about 2 minutes. Stir in the smoked paprika, cumin, anise seeds, capers, olives, and parsley. Season with salt

(continued)

1 cup finely chopped red onion

1 cup canned tomatoes (2 to 3 whole canned San Marzano–style tomatoes, chopped by hand)

1 tablespoon smoked paprika

1 tablespoon ground cumin

1 tablespoon ground anise seeds

1 tablespoon capers in brine, drained and finely chopped

10 green olives with (or without) pimento stuffing, drained and finely chopped

1 tablespoon finely chopped fresh parsley

Salt and freshly ground black pepper

2 hard-boiled eggs, diced

FOR SERVING:

½ cup Chimichurri Sauce (page 163)

Tomato powder (page 188, optional)

and pepper. Reduce the heat to low, return the meat to the pan, stir in the hard-boiled eggs, and heat just until warm. Remove the filling from the heat, transfer to a large bowl, and refrigerate until cooled, about 15 minutes.

TO MAKE THE EMPANADAS: While the filling is cooling, preheat the oven to 350°F and line a baking sheet with parchment paper.

Remove the dough from the refrigerator and separate it into golf ball–sized spheres. Take a gallon zip-top-style freezer bag, cut the top off, and open each of the sides. Place the bag in a tortilla press, the open side out, and place a dough ball in the middle of the bag. Press the ball into a flat disk. Add 1 to 2 tablespoons of filling in the center and fold the circle into a half-moon. Pinch and fold the edges to seal them (crimping with a fork if you like). Transfer the empanadas to the prepared baking sheet. Continue with the remaining dough and filling. Brush the completed empanadas with egg wash, transfer to the oven, and bake until golden brown, approximately 20 to 25 minutes.

TO SERVE: Swipe a pool of chimichurri sauce across each plate and top with one or two empanadas. Dust with tomato powder.

LARGE PLATES

For at least one full generation, American views on food—particularly "good" food—have been shaped by food television. From *Emeril Live* and *Iron Chef America* to *Chopped*, our ideas of how to cook and our culinary aspirations have been captured by these shows, their catchphrases, and "rules." But a weeknight supper isn't *Top Chef*, is it? So there's no reason not to make risotto.

The reason no one ever wins with risotto is, frankly, exactly what makes risotto so good: time. That, plus patience, the right kind of rice (Arborio is the best variety readily available), and a few basic concepts yields a dish that's creamy without any cream, rich yet not necessarily fattening, devilish but simple, and soft yet toothsome.

The basic idea is to add the broth so that the rice absorbs it gradually, loosening the starch in the rice to yield the characteristic creaminess of the dish. But it's easy to go too far or fast with the liquid. It shouldn't be mushy. On the contrary, the grains must retain a little "bite," a firmness and individuality for each grain. Add the broth too fast, before the rice has absorbed the last batch, and the result is a gooey, porridge-like mess. The key is to add just enough liquid to cover the rice and stir constantly, letting it fully absorb before adding more.

RISOTTO OF MUSHROOMS AND PEAS WITH TOMATO CONFIT

SERVES 4—OR DOUBLE THE RECIPE AND SAVE 2 CUPS FOR ARANCINI (PAGE 91)

4 tablespoons extra-virgin olive oil

1 pound mixed mushrooms (white button, cremini, maitake), cut into even-sized pieces

Salt

4 cups Mushroom Stock (page 156)

2 large shallots (or ½ small red onion), finely chopped

1 tablespoon finely minced fennel bulb

2 cups Arborio rice

1 cup very dry, unoaked white wine (such as sauvignon blanc or pinot grigio)

1 ounce dried porcini mushrooms, soaked in 2 to 3 cups of hot water

1 tablespoon fresh thyme leaves

Heat 2 tablespoons of the olive oil in large skillet over medium-high heat. Add the mixed mushrooms and season with salt. Cook until tender and beginning to brown, 3 to 4 minutes. Transfer to a bowl and hold on the side.

Bring the stock to a boil in a medium saucepan and immediately reduce the heat to maintain a simmer. In a heavy, medium pot, heat the remaining 2 tablespoons olive oil over medium-high heat, add the shallots, and cook until they turn translucent, 2 to 3 minutes. Add the fennel and cook for 1 minute. Add the rice and stir well, just toasting it.

Add ½ cup wine to the pan with the rice and cook, stirring, until most of the liquid is absorbed by the rice. Do the same with the stock. Alternate adding ¼ cup of the wine with adding ¼ cup of the stock until all of the wine and half of the stock has been absorbed (you should still have 2 cups of stock), stirring constantly all the while.

(continued)

1 cup frozen peas

½ cup grated Parmesan or Romano cheese

4 cherry tomatoes from Tomato Confit (page 193)

Parsley leaves, for garnish

Strain the porcini mushrooms, discarding the liquid, and finely chop the rehydrated porcinis. Add them, along with the cooked mushrooms, to the pan and cook, stirring, until incorporated, about 1 minute. Turn the heat down to low and add the thyme. Cook, stirring, until fragrant, about 30 seconds. Taste and adjust the seasonings.

Test the doneness on the rice. The rice should be fully cooked but not mushy. It must remain al dente with each grain distinct but the whole dish creamy. If it is not done, continue cooking and adding stock. When it is nearly finished, add the peas and cook for a minute longer. Add the grated cheese and mix to combine. When the cheese is melted, fold to mix thoroughly with the mushroom mixture. Season with salt and let the dish rest for a minute or two to cool and thicken.

Spoon the risotto into a ring mold set on top of a plate. Using the bottom of a wine glass, a spoon, or spatula, compress the risotto gently, just barely enough to make it stay in place. Some of the creamy liquid will seep out the bottom—a sign of the deliciousness to come. Spoon 1 confit tomato on top. Arrange parsley on top of the tomato confit. Repeat with the remaining risotto.

Traditionally, carbonara is pasta with egg, hard cheese, *guanciale* (or pancetta or prosciutto), and black pepper. Sweet peas are a frequent addition that I chose to include here for the sweetness and freshness they add to the dish. Because guanciale, pancetta, and prosciutto are pork products, of course, traditional carbonara is not kosher.

But when you look at the role guanciale plays in the dish, it really comes down to one word—umami. There are other ways to get the sort of umami those pork products bring to the party, one of the best being oven-dried tomatoes, which bring a similar depth of flavor and a similar savory profile as the cured pork.

Carbonara is classically made with bucatini or spaghetti, but I love making it with penne pasta. Why? Because the little bits—the peas and oven-dried tomatoes in this recipe—get stuck in the tubes of penne. But you can use whichever shape you prefer.

PENNE "CARBONARA" WITH SWEET PEAS AND OVEN-DRIED TOMATOES

SERVES 4 TO 6

Salt

1 pound dry penne

3 tablespoons extra-virgin olive oil

¼ pound Oven-Dried Tomatoes (page 188), sliced into small strips

4 cloves garlic, finely chopped

1 cup frozen sweet peas, thawed

2 large eggs

1 cup freshly grated Pecorino Romano cheese (plus more for serving)

1 handful fresh parsley, chopped

Bring a large pot of salted water to a boil, add the pasta, and cook for 8 to 10 minutes, to the point that the pasta is al dente. Drain the pasta well, reserving at least ½ cup of the starchy cooking water to use in the sauce.

Meanwhile, heat 2 tablespoons of the olive oil in a deep skillet over medium heat. Add the oven-dried tomatoes to the pan, increase the heat to high, and cook for about 2 minutes, until the tomatoes are slightly caramelized. Turn the heat down to medium, add the garlic and sweet peas, and cook for another 2 minutes.

Beat the eggs and cheese together in a medium bowl, stirring well to prevent lumps. Add the hot, drained pasta to the pan along with the remaining 1 tablespoon olive oil and toss to coat the pasta. Reduce the heat to maintain a simmer and pour the egg mixture into the pasta, mixing quickly until the eggs thicken but do not scramble (it is lower risk to do this off the heat, but the results will never be as good). Thin out the sauce with a bit of the reserved pasta water, until it just clings to the pasta. Taste the dish and adjust the seasoning.

Divide the carbonara among plates and garnish with the parsley.

I f you can build a sandcastle, you can make this dish. It is pretty much just piling a bunch of things on top of each other in a repeated pattern. If making the ricotta is more than you want to do on a Tuesday night, don't do it—go buy ricotta and enjoy. You'll probably want to go to an Italian market or a high-end supermarket to get your fresh pasta sheets, so you're there already.

The key to this dish is the mint-pepita pesto. It gives the dish both brightness and a depth of flavor. For a little more of that, do not hesitate to add a bit of Garum (page 169). You might want to make some extra pesto and freeze it. It makes an excellent pasta sauce for an easy night's dinner.

LASAGNETTE OF MUSHROOMS, HOUSE-MADE RICOTTA, AND MINT-PEPITA PESTO

SERVES 4

1 package fresh lasagna noodles (cut into sixteen 1½ x 3½-inch rectangles)

FOR THE RICOTTA:

4 cups whole milk

½ teaspoon salt

3 tablespoons distilled vinegar

FOR THE MUSHROOM FILLING:

3 tablespoons butter

2 tablespoons extra-virgin olive oil (plus more for brushing)

1½ pounds cremini mushrooms (or button mushrooms), sliced

1 cup (about 8 ounces) dried mushrooms (shiitake, porcini, morel), rehydrated and squeezed dry

Salt

1 large shallot, finely chopped

⅓ cup dry white wine (such as pinot grigio)

FOR THE MINT-PEPITA PESTO:

2 small cloves garlic, crushed

⅔ cup fresh mint leaves

½ cup raw pumpkin seeds (pepitas)

¼ teaspoon salt

½ cup extra-virgin olive oil

TO MAKE THE RICOTTA: Pour the milk into a heavy-bottomed pot. Add the salt and heat over medium heat, stirring occasionally so the milk doesn't scorch, until the milk reaches 180°F on an instant-read or deep-fry thermometer (the milk will start to foam at the edges of the pan and may simmer but shouldn't boil). Remove the pan from the heat and add vinegar, stirring until curds start to form.

Line a medium sieve with cheesecloth and carefully pour the milk mixture through the sieve, disturbing the curds as little as possible. Let drain for anywhere from 20 minutes to 1 hour to achieve a relatively firm ricotta. How firm (and thus how long you want to let it continue to drain) is entirely a matter of personal preference. Cool the ricotta to room temperature, then cover and refrigerate for up to 4 days.

TO MAKE THE MUSHROOM FILLING: Melt 2 tablespoons of the butter in the olive oil in a large skillet over medium-high heat. Add the mushrooms, season with salt, and cook, stirring occasionally, until browned and starting to crisp, 8 to 10 minutes. Add the shallot, wine, and the remaining 1 tablespoon butter. Cook, stirring occasionally, until the skillet is dry, about 5 minutes. Test the seasoning on the mushrooms and adjust accordingly. Transfer the mushroom mixture to a large bowl and set aside.

TO MAKE THE MINT-PEPITA PESTO: Preheat the oven to 350°F.

(continued)

Combine the garlic, mint leaves, pumpkin seeds, salt, and 1 tablespoon of the olive oil in a food processor and pulse to combine. With processor running, slowly add the remaining oil in a slow, steady stream until completely used. This can be made ahead and stored in an airtight container in the refrigerator for up to 1 week. When ready to use, bring it out of the refrigerator and back to room temperature before using.

TO ASSEMBLE AND BAKE THE LASAGNETTE: Line a baking sheet with parchment paper (or use a large lasagna pan). Spread four thin rectangles of ricotta around the pan and top each with a pasta sheet. These are the glue on which you will build each of your lasagnette stacks. Place a pasta segment on top of each rectangle of ricotta as the bottom layer of the lasagnette. Spread a large spoonful of ricotta over the pasta, then scatter some mushrooms over the top of the ricotta. For your next layer, spread a large spoonful of the pesto on a pasta segment and place that—pesto-side down—on top of the mushroom layer.

Repeat the layering process (starting with the noodles and ending with dropping the pesto side of the sheet on the mushrooms) twice more. Cover the lasagnette with foil and bake until warmed through, 10 to 15 minutes. Remove the foil and continue baking until golden brown, 15 to 20 minutes. Let cool for at least 5 minutes up to 10 minutes. Garnish each lasagnette with an attractive mint leaf.

No dish speaks of California's "Barbary Coast" quite as strongly as cioppino, a rich, to-mato-based seafood stew that originated as a classic fisherman's meal similar to its cousins from Mediterranean regions such as *cacciucco* or *brodetto* from Italy, bouilla-baisse or bourride from France, or *suquet de peix* from Catalonia. It has been said that cioppino can trace its origins to Genoa on Italy's Ligurian coast, the town of origin of many of the Italian fishermen who settled in San Francisco's North Beach district. It would catch on up and down California's coast.

As it evolved into its current form, however, it seemed that modern cioppino had to involve California's signature Dungeness crab as well as other nonkosher shellfish and crustaceans. But as I thought about what I love most in cioppino, I realized it lay more in its Old World, fisherman's "catch of the day" origins. At the core of the dish, viewed that way, are the tomato-garlic-wine-based broth and use of the freshest, most plentiful, and best available fish.

When each bowl is presented with a crouton topped with the aioli-like Mayonnaise (page 168), it's a bit of a nod to Provençal bourride.

CALIFORNIA FISHERMAN'S CIOPPINO

SERVES 4 TO 6

1 large onion, finely chopped

2 leeks, white parts only, cleaned and finely chopped

2 bulbs fennel, cored and diced (fronds and stalks reserved for another purpose)

2 tablespoons extra-virgin olive oil

1 (28-ounce) can diced tomatoes with their juices

2 cups Fish Stock (page 157)

2 cups Chicken Stock (page 151)

2 cups dry white wine (such as unoaked California chardonnay)

3 cloves garlic, crushed

Juice of 2 lemons

1 tablespoon Worcestershire sauce

2 bay leaves

1 tablespoon minced fresh basil

1 tablespoon minced fresh oregano (or marjoram)

½ to 1 teaspoon red chile flakes

3 pounds of a variety of very fresh fish (such as halibut, grouper, sea bass, and/or red snapper), boned and cut into 1-inch cubes

4 to 6 Croutons (page 197) (plus more for passing)

1 to 2 tablespoons Mayonnaise (page 168)

¼ cup chopped fresh parsley

In a large soup pot, sweat the onion, leeks, and fennel in the olive oil over low heat until the onion turns translucent, about 5 minutes. Add the toma-toes, both stocks, the wine, garlic, lemon juice, Worcestershire sauce, bay leaves, basil, oregano, and red chile flakes to taste to the soup pot and bring to a boil over high heat. Reduce the heat to low and simmer, uncovered, for 30 to 45 minutes, until the flavors come together.

Add the fish to the stew, raise the heat to medi-um-high, and bring to a boil, then reduce the heat and simmer, uncovered, until the fish is cooked through, about another 5 minutes.

Ladle the stew into large bowls, place a crouton topped with a little dollop of the mayonnaise in each bowl, and garnish with the parsley.

*A*ushak is the national dish of Afghanistan. As a major stop on the Silk Road—the ancient trade routes between Europe and China—Afghanistan necessarily reached its arms both east and west. Its culture and its food took something from both, never fully assimilating either. Aushak, like many Afghani dishes, shows that heritage—with the dumplings feeling like one-part Italian ravioli, one-part Chinese *jiaozi*.

But, like many Middle Eastern dishes, traditional aushak combines yogurt (for creaminess) with meat (for richness and savory character). By substituting a rich mushroom duxelles for the ground beef of the original recipe, however, a fully kosher dairy-based dish results. While this version of aushak is certainly different than the classic—lighter, more umami-forward—it is every bit as rich and tasty.

AUSHAK WITH DUXELLES
SERVES 6

FOR THE DUXELLES:

½ pound white mushrooms

2 teaspoons butter

1 teaspoon canola oil

2 tablespoons finely minced shallot

1 tablespoon dry sherry

Salt

½ teaspoon freshly grated nutmeg

FOR THE AUSHAK:

2 leeks, white parts only, cleaned and finely chopped

⅓ teaspoon red chile flakes

1 tablespoon extra-virgin olive oil

Salt

24 square wonton wrappers (such as Gefen or Twin Marquis)

All-purpose flour

TO MAKE THE DUXELLES: Roughly chop the mushrooms, place them in the bowl of a food processor, pulse a few times to break the mushrooms down, then process until finely minced. Transfer to a square of cheesecloth, wrap, and wring out the liquid. The result should be a nearly solid lump of chopped mushrooms. Melt the butter in the canola oil in a medium sauté pan over medium heat and heat until the foam subsides. Add the shallots and cook until they just turn translucent, about 1 minute. Add the mushrooms and cook, stirring often, until they begin to brown and there is almost no liquid remaining, 5 to 6 minutes. Stir in the sherry and cook until evaporated. Add the salt and nutmeg.

TO MAKE THE AUSHAK: In a small sauté pan, cook the leeks with the chile flakes in the olive oil over medium heat until the leeks are translucent, about 2 minutes. Add the salt.

Fill a small bowl with cold water. Starting with 1 wonton wrapper on a lightly floured surface, spoon 2 teaspoons of the leeks into the center and brush the circumference of the wrapper with water. Fold one corner of the wonton wrapper over the filling to form a triangle, pressing down around the filling carefully to force out any air. Seal the edges and trim the excess dough around the filling, leaving an apron of about ¼ inch. Repeat with the remaining wrappers and leek filling. As they are formed, transfer the aushak to a plate, spread a little flour between the dumplings to keep them from sticking, and cover with a dry kitchen towel, turning them occasionally.

FOR THE CHAKAH (YOGURT SAUCE):

2 cups plain Greek yogurt

2 cloves garlic, minced

1 teaspoon salt

FOR COOKING AND GARNISHING:

Salt

1 tablespoon extra-virgin olive oil

2 to 3 teaspoons dried mint, ground to a powder in a spice/coffee grinder

TO MAKE THE CHAKAH: Combine the yogurt, garlic, and salt in the bowl of a food processor and pulse to mix. Set aside.

TO COOK THE AUSHAK AND SERVE: In a large pot, bring 8 cups of water to a boil and add the salt and oil. Carefully drop the aushak into the water and cook until tender, about 3 minutes. Ladle a circle of the chakah onto each plate. Remove the aushak with a slotted spoon directly to the top of the chakah on each plate. Top with the duxelles, and sprinkle with the powdered mint.

The long list of famed kosher Mexican dishes is a short one. It's not because Mexican cuisine is inherently incompatible with the laws of kashrut. Rather, it's because what Americans think of as "Mexican" cuisine is really either (a) *antojitos* (essentially a small plate snack or street food) often pairing meat and cheese or (b) pork or shellfish dishes. One of the best and most famous of the latter is pozole, a pre-Hispanic hominy stew, most commonly made with pork and flavored with chiles and a set of iconic garnishes.

But there are pozoles in Mexico that don't include pork—chicken is not uncommon and there are versions with shrimp and fish as well. For this recipe, I swapped duck in for the pork. The richness of the fowl pairs even better with the red chile–flavored broth (with its hints of fruit and acidity) than does the original treif. Is it a straight-up improvement? This recipe retains, of course, the wonderful garnishes and hence the fun of passing them around the table allowing each diner to pick and choose the ones they want.

DUCK POZOLE ROJO

SERVES 4 TO 6

FOR THE BROTH:

1 duck carcass (breasts reserved for another purpose) plus 2 extra duck legs (or 10 duck legs) (about 5 pounds total) skinned

1 medium onion, roughly chopped

1 medium carrot, roughly chopped

1 large (or 2 small) ribs celery, chopped

3 cloves garlic, crushed

2 bay leaves

6 cups Chicken Stock (page 151)

5 dried guajillo chiles

2 dried ancho chiles

1 (30-ounce) can hominy, rinsed and drained

FOR THE GARNISH:

Shredded green cabbage

Thinly sliced red radishes

1 medium onion, diced

Fresh cilantro leaves

Dried Mexican oregano

Arbol chiles

Lime wedges

Preheat the oven to 400°F and line a baking sheet with parchment paper.

Chop the duck carcass (don't forget the neck). You can ask your butcher to do this, but it's great stress relief to do it yourself and not difficult. Roast the duck carcass on the prepared baking sheet in the oven until it starts to brown, about 30 to 45 minutes. (Do the same if using only legs.) Add the roasted duck parts to a stockpot along with the onion, carrot, celery, garlic, bay leaves, and stock and bring to a boil over high heat. Reduce the heat to maintain a simmer and cook for at least 45 minutes (the longer the better), until the stock takes on a rich duck flavor. Strain the stock into a soup pot, removing the duck carcass and legs with tongs to cool.

Meanwhile, preheat a large sauté pan over medium heat. Cut the stems off the guajillo and ancho chiles, removing the seeds as you do so. Toast the chiles in the pan until they just begin to develop dark marks, about 30 seconds. Flip the chiles and toast their other sides. Soak the chiles in a bowl with hot water to cover for 30 minutes, or until they are tender and pliable. Remove them and add to the bowl of a high-speed blender or food processor along with ¼ cup of the duck stock and process to a smooth paste, about 30 seconds.

(continued)

Once the duck legs are cool enough to handle, remove and discard the bones and shred the meat into bite-sized pieces. Add the shredded duck, chile purée, and hominy to the soup pot with the duck broth and bring to a boil. Reduce the heat to maintain a simmer and cook the broth for 20 minutes to marry all the flavors. Again, taste the pozole to test for seasoning and adjust accordingly (if it needs more acidity, add some lime juice).

Ladle the pozole into soup bowls and serve with the garnishes alongside.

uck breast is one of my favorite ingredients. When done right—seared with the skin all crispy, fat rendered, and lusciously rare in the middle—they are glorious. Home cooks, though, are often intimidated by duck breasts. How do you get the skin crisp but not burnt and the fat rendered, without cooking the meat to death?

The answer lies in a trick from Gordon Ramsay: Start the cooking skin-side down in a cold pan that you gradually bring up to heat, letting the fat render out from underneath the skin.

This dish is a play on the classic *duck à l'orange*. The classic can trend a little too far to the sweet end of the spectrum for my tastes, and the traditional use of butter seems unnecessary (and is nonkosher) given the duck's naturally delicious fat. The sour orange sauce takes the classic in a different direction; one that helps cut the duck's fattiness. Pairing that duck with the Padrón peppers of Spain's Galicia region yields a well-balanced dish. Eating Padrón peppers is a bit of a lottery. Most are very mild, but every once in a while you get a spicy one (that is still less spicy than a jalapeño). This isn't just a matter of which plant the peppers are taken from—the same plant will produce one spicy pepper while all the rest are mild.

PAN-ROASTED DUCK BREAST WITH PADRÓN PEPPERS AND SOUR ORANGE SAUCE

SERVES 4

FOR THE SOUR ORANGE REDUCTION:

1 medium shallot, finely chopped

1 cup orange juice

1 tablespoon fresh lemon juice

1 cup Chicken Stock (page 151)

Kosher salt and freshly ground black pepper

FOR THE DUCK BREASTS:

2 duck breasts, 8 to 10 ounces each

Kosher salt and freshly ground black pepper

TO MAKE THE SOUR ORANGE REDUCTION: Combine the shallot, orange juice, and lemon juice in a medium saucepan and bring to a boil. Turn the heat down and simmer until reduced by half, about 15 to 20 minutes. Add the chicken stock and bring back to a boil, then turn the heat down and reduce the sauce until it just coats the back of a spoon, 20 to 30 minutes depending on your specific equipment (stove and pots). Season to taste with salt and pepper.

TO COOK THE DUCK BREASTS: While the sauce is cooking, preheat the oven to 400°F.

Score the skin of the duck breasts carefully (be certain not to cut into the flesh of the meat), creating a diagonal checkerboard pattern. Season the duck breasts liberally, on both sides, with kosher salt and pepper. Place the duck breasts skin-side down on an oven-proof sauté pan (without oil). Cook, gradually turning the heat up to medium over the course of 5 minutes or so, until the fat from the scored skin almost completely renders, running out into the pan.

(continued)

FOR THE PADRÓN PEPPERS:

1 tablespoon grapeseed, canola, or another neutral oil

1 pound Padrón (or shishito) peppers

Maldon salt (or other flaky finishing salt)

Turn the heat up to high and continue to sear until the skin gets golden brown, about another minute. Flip the breasts to the flesh side for 1 minute, then transfer the pan to the oven and roast the breasts, skin-side down, for 6 to 8 minutes, until the flesh gives a little resistance but still gives to the finger when poked. Remove the duck breasts from the pan and rest them for 5 minutes before slicing. The breasts should be medium-rare.

TO MAKE THE PADRÓN PEPPERS: While the duck is roasting, heat the oil in a large sauté pan over high heat until just smoking. Add the peppers and cook, tossing occasionally, until the skins are blistered and the flesh is softened, about 4 minutes. Transfer to a bowl, sprinkle with Maldon salt, and toss to coat.

TO SERVE: Pour a line of the sauce horizontally across the plate. Arrange a few slices of duck per plate over the sauce, some skin-side up, others with the cut surface up, leaving a few gaps here and there. Fill the gaps with the blistered peppers.

At first blush this dish may read as a Moroccan tagine or another classic North African stew. It was, no doubt, inspired by those. What it really is, though, is a dish based on classic combinations of flavors in new permutations rather than on any particular recipe. The key is the balance between salty, sweet, sour, and savory along with some funk. It is, pretty much, something of an old classic dish that I just made up. That makes it a lot like many dishes in New Israeli cuisine.

This recipe calls for the veal stew to be served over couscous. It's delicious that way. But there is really no reason you couldn't serve it over rice or stuffed in pita. It's not like your grandmother is going to be offended by such changes in an old family heirloom recipe.

VEAL STEW WITH PRESERVED LEMON, OLIVES, AND CHARRED TOMATO-OIL SCALLIONS

SERVES 4

2 tablespoons extra-virgin olive oil

2 pounds veal shoulder, trimmed and cut into 2-inch pieces

Salt and freshly ground black pepper

2 tablespoons Baharat Spice Blend (page 183)

1 large onion, diced

1 large leek, white parts only, cleaned, halved lengthwise, and thinly sliced across

1 medium carrot, diced

1 bulb fennel, cored and diced (fronds and stalks reserved for another purpose)

3 cloves garlic, peeled and crushed

1 dried red chile (árbol or Japanese), crumbled (or ½ teaspoon red chile flakes)

2 bay leaves

3 sprigs thyme

2 tablespoons chopped fresh parsley

Heat the olive oil in a large sauté pan over high heat. Season the veal aggressively with salt and pepper. Once the oil is hot, working in batches to avoid crowding the pan, add the veal to the pan and brown on all sides, about 8 minutes per batch, then remove it from the pan and set aside. Pour off any excess oil, leaving the fond in the pan. Add the Baharat spices, onion, leek, carrot, fennel, garlic, chiles, bay leaves, thyme, and parsley and sweat the vegetables until they give up their water, about three to four minutes, deglazing by scraping the fond from the pan using the moisture released by the vegetables.

Transfer the contents of the pan to a large Dutch oven. Add the tomatoes and stock, stir well, return the meat to the Dutch oven, add the wine, and bring to a boil. Reduce the heat and simmer over the lowest heat possible until the meat is soft and falling apart, about 2 hours.

Meanwhile, marinate the scallion whites in the tomato oil for at least 30 minutes up to an hour. After the stew has cooked for 2 hours, add the olives and preserved lemon slices and cook for an additional 15 to 20 minutes.

While the stew is going through the final cook, prepare the couscous in accordance with the package's instructions.

(continued)

1 (16-ounce) can peeled plum tomatoes

1 cup Chicken Stock (page 151)

½ cup dry white wine (such as a white Rhône or Provençal Marsanne)

12 scallions, white parts cut in 1½- to 2-inch sections, greens finely chopped

¼ cup tomato oil from Tomato Confit (page 193)

20 oil-cured black olives

2 preserved lemons (or Quick Preserved Lemons; page 179), well rinsed and thinly sliced

2 cups fine-grain couscous

Meanwhile, strain the scallion segments. Reserve 1 tablespoon confit oil from the marinating scallion whites. Heat a medium-sized sauté pan over high heat until extremely hot, add the remaining 3 tablespoons oil, and swirl to spread. Add the marinated scallions and char, exposing different surfaces of the scallions so as to create multiple marks.

Spoon ½ cup of the couscous in each of four bowls and top with the veal stew. Arrange the charred scallion whites around it and garnish with the scallion greens.

Veal piccata is a traditional Italian dish of thin-pounded veal cutlets in a sauce of lemon juice, chicken stock, capers, and parsley. Classically, butter does double duty as both a thickener for the sauce and a flavoring ingredient. Swap in schmaltz for the butter, though, and—at least arguably—the former works better than the latter. The meatiness of the schmaltz ties together the lemon and the veal.

VEAL PICCATA

SERVES 4

2 pounds veal cutlets (about 12 pieces), pounded ¼ inch thick

Salt and freshly ground black pepper

½ cup all-purpose flour

6 tablespoons Schmaltz (page 187)

½ cup dry white wine (such as pinot grigio)

1¼ cups Chicken Stock (page 151)

1 tablespoon fresh lemon juice (plus more to taste)

¼ cup capers in brine, drained

2 tablespoons chopped fresh parsley

Zest of 1 lemon

Season the veal cutlets with salt and pepper and dredge in the flour, shaking off any excess. Heat 2 tablespoons of the schmaltz in a large sauté pan over medium-high heat. Working in batches, add the veal and cook, turning only once, until the cutlets are golden brown, about 3 minutes total. Transfer the cooked veal to a platter and set aside.

Add the wine to the pan and cook, scraping the bottom of pan, until reduced by half, about 3 minutes. Add the stock, bring to a boil over high heat, and continue cooking until reduced by half, about 8 minutes. Add the remaining 4 tablespoons schmaltz, 1 tablespoon of the lemon juice, and the capers. Taste the sauce and adjust the seasoning by adding salt or lemon juice (keeping in mind you will garnish with lemon zest). Strain the sauce through a fine-mesh strainer, reserving the solids for garnish.

Arrange three pieces of veal per plate. Spoon the sauce over the veal and garnish with the capers, parsley, and lemon zest.

The elegance of lamb, of course, invites fancy sauces. The problem is that the sauces often fight with or mask the very thing that attracts me most to lamb: the flavor of the meat. I prefer to go a different direction. Instead, I use the funky, earthy flavors of anchovy and capers, garlic, black pepper, and grassy parsley found in an Italian *salsa verde*—a sauce Joyce Goldstein observed in her terrific book on Italian Jewish cuisine, *Cucina Ebraica*, is of Jewish origin—to complement the meat's richness.

PAN-ROASTED LAMB CHOPS WITH ITALIAN SALSA VERDE

SERVES 4 TO 6

FOR THE LAMB CHOPS:

1 rack of lamb (about 2 pounds), Frenched

Salt and freshly ground black pepper

2 tablespoons grapeseed, canola, or another neutral oil

FOR THE ITALIAN SALSA VERDE:

1½ cups packed roughly chopped fresh parsley

⅔ cup extra-virgin olive oil (plus more as needed)

¼ cup capers in brine, drained

3 anchovy fillets, rinsed

1 tablespoon white wine vinegar

2 medium cloves garlic, minced (about 2 teaspoons)

½ teaspoon freshly grated lemon zest (from 1 lemon)

1 to 2 tablespoons fresh lemon juice

Salt and freshly ground black pepper

FOR THE GARNISH:

Red Pepper Skin Curls (page 196; optional)

Finishing salt

TO SEASON THE LAMB: Season the lamb rack liberally with salt and pepper. Let rest for 30 minutes at room temperature. Preheat the oven to 350°F.

TO MAKE THE SALSA VERDE: While the lamb is resting, combine the parsley, olive oil, capers, anchovies, vinegar, garlic, lemon zest, and 1 tablespoon of the lemon juice in the bowl of a high-speed blender or food processor. Start on low speed (or pulse until the parsley is well chopped), then gradually increase the speed. Scrape down the sides of the bowl several times, then increase the speed and blend until the ingredients achieve a smooth, silky consistency.

TO COOK THE LAMB: Heat a large, heavy ovenproof sauté pan over high heat. When hot, add the grapeseed oil and sear the lamb until nicely browned, about 3 minutes per side (flip the racks using tongs). Place the rack in the oven and cook to an internal temperature of 145°F (for medium-rare), about 10 minutes. Remove the rack of lamb from the oven and let stand.

TO FINISH THE DISH AND SERVE: While the lamb is resting, season the sauce with salt and pepper. Adjust the acidity by adding some extra lemon juice or oil as needed. Cut the rack into individual chops.

Spoon 2 to 3 tablespoons of the sauce onto each plate. With a palette knife or the back of a spoon, swipe sauce across the plate in an arc. Plate 3 chops, with bones crossed, in the sauce, then sprinkle with red pepper curls and finishing salt.

Of the many wonderful things to be found in Spain, the traditional home of Sephardic Jews—including the architecture, art, music, and fashion—the greatest has to be the food. And as much as I love and appreciate Spain's *alta cocina*, the truest expression of Spain's culinary culture is its myriad tapas. The creativity of the tapas bars of San Sebastian, Madrid, and Barcelona cannot be topped, no doubt. But there is something special about tapas in Seville, where it all began.

My favorite tapa on our trip to Seville was a very simple, very elegant, and deeply flavored little bowl of oxtail stew we tasted in Santa Cruz, Seville's old Jewish Quarter. In addition to being the home of tapas, Andalusia is also the home to bullfighting. One tradition in Spain is that wherever there's a big bullring, there's a restaurant that serves the bull's tail (the *rabo* of the *toro*) after the fight. Braising the oxtails in one of Andalusia's other great exports (sherry) brings out the savory succulence and incredible tenderness that time and patience reveal in this seemingly tough ingredient. The chive buds—an ingredient readily available at Asian markets—is an elegant and tasty garnish. They are, however, purely optional.

For the contemporary version I braise the oxtails in the traditional ingredients but, after refrigerating the oxtails in the braising liquid overnight, I defat then strain the broth before clarifying it. The result is a clean and clear broth with dramatic oxtails and simple garnishes.

SEVILLA-STYLE "RABO DE TORO" (OXTAIL STEW)

SERVES 2 TO 4

4 large oxtail segments (3 to 4 pounds total)

Salt and freshly ground black pepper

All-purpose flour for dusting

2 tablespoons extra-virgin olive oil, divided

2 leeks, white parts only, cleaned, halved lengthwise, and thinly sliced across

1 large onion, chopped

1 large carrot, chopped

1 green bell pepper, chopped

3 medium tomatoes, chopped

4 cups Beef Stock (page 152)

1 cup dry sherry (fino or Manzanilla)

2 bay leaves

4 large egg whites

4 chive buds (optional)

Season the oxtails with salt and pepper and sprinkle with flour to create a light dusting. Heat 1 tablespoon olive oil in a large soup pot or Dutch oven over high heat. Working in batches, sear the oxtails until evenly browned, about 30 seconds per side, then transfer them to a plate.

Heat the second tablespoon of the olive oil in the same pot over medium-low heat, then stir in the leeks, onion, and carrot and sweat the vegetables just until the onion turns translucent, stirring all the while to deglaze the pan with the liquids from the vegetables, about 5 minutes. Stir in the bell pepper and tomatoes and cook until they lose their texture, about another 10 minutes.

Return the oxtails to the pot along with the beef stock and sherry and bring to a boil over high heat. Add the bay leaves. When the liquid comes to a boil, reduce the heat to low and simmer until the

(continued)

oxtails are tender, about 3 hours. Remove the oxtails from the broth and pour the broth through a conical or fine-mesh strainer into a large bowl, pressing on the solids to extract as much liquid as possible. Discard the solids. Return the oxtails to the broth, let it cool, then cover and transfer to the refrigerator and refrigerate overnight.

The next day, skim the fat from the top of the broth, then remove the oxtails to a plate. Transfer the chilled stock to a medium pot. Place the egg whites in a medium bowl and whip until just starting to foam. Whisk the beaten egg whites into the broth and set over medium heat. Bring the broth just to a gentle simmer, stirring occasionally, but don't let it reach a full boil. A "raft" will appear on the surface as the proteins in the egg whites coagulate—you'll know it when you see it. This raft is the engine that cleanses the broth by gathering the impurities. As this happens, stop stirring and let the broth simmer gently for about 30 minutes, adjusting the heat to keep it below a full boil.

Carefully agitate the bottom of the pot with a spatula to loosen any raft that may be caught. Simmer the broth gently for about 5 minutes, breaking the surface of the raft as necessary to allow some of the pressure to escape. When the raft is solid and you can no longer see impurities rising to the surface, remove the pan from the heat. Using a ladle, pass the clear liquid off through a fine-mesh strainer into another soup pot, transfer the oxtails to the new pot, and reheat the clarified broth and oxtails over medium heat for 5 to 10 minutes.

To serve, arrange 1 to 2 oxtails in the bottom of each soup bowl and ladle the broth over. Garnish each oxtail with a chive bud.

There are many different ways to cook a steak. They range from a quick cook on the backyard charcoal grill to a precision vacuum-sealed bath in a sous-vide setup followed by a quick sear. I like them all (although I do consider "well-done steak" an oxymoron).

But my favorite may be the reverse-sear technique. Instead of searing first and then finishing the steak in the oven, you cook the steak in a low-heat oven and then finish it in a piping hot pan to get that beautiful caramelized crust.

One key to this method is patience with the first part: the low temperature cook. Cook the steak at no higher than 225°F. It's crucial to the final result to bring the interior of the steak up to speed slowly. If the cook time is too long for your taste or time at 225°F, then use another technique.

NEW YORK STRIP STEAK WITH MUSHROOM AND RED WINE REDUCTION

SERVES 4

FOR THE STEAKS:

4 (12- to 16-ounce) New York strip steaks, between 1½ and 2 inches thick

Salt and freshly ground black pepper

1 tablespoon grapeseed, canola, or another neutral oil

1 tablespoon Schmaltz (page 187)

FOR THE MUSHROOM AND RED WINE REDUCTION:

2 tablespoons Schmaltz (page 187)

½ pound cremini or white mushrooms, sliced

1 teaspoon minced fresh rosemary

Salt and freshly ground black pepper

½ cup dry red wine (such as cabernet sauvignon)

¾ cup Beef Stock (page 152)

1 teaspoon cornstarch

FOR THE GARNISH:

Pink Pickled Onions (page 177)

Finishing salt (such as Maldon salt)

TO SEASON AND COOK THE STEAKS: Season the steaks liberally with salt and pepper. If possible, do this the night before and let them rest in the refrigerator overnight. Salting an hour before and leaving them to rest at room temperature is also perfectly acceptable and can still make a great steak.

Preheat the oven to 225°F.

Set the steaks on a wire rack set on a rimmed baking sheet. Transfer to the oven and cook until an instant-read thermometer registers 105°F for rare, 115°F for medium-rare, 125°F for medium, or 135°F for medium-well. It will take about 20 minutes for rare steak and up to about 40 minutes for medium-well. Check the internal temperature frequently because it can rise quickly. The higher the internal temperature gets, the faster they increase. If you want to go beyond medium-well, knock yourself out, but I don't want to be complicit by telling you a temperature.

TO MAKE THE MUSHROOM AND RED WINE REDUCTION: Meanwhile, melt the schmaltz in a medium skillet over medium-high heat. Add the mushrooms and minced rosemary and season with salt and pepper. Cook until the mushrooms are browned on both sides, 6 to 10 minutes (depending mostly on their water content). Add the wine, beef stock, and cornstarch and cook, stirring occasionally, until reduced by half, 3 to 4 minutes.

(continued)

TO FINISH THE STEAKS AND SERVE: Remove the steaks from the oven and rest them for 10 to 15 minutes under foil. Heat the oil with the schmaltz in a large, heavy sauté pan (cast iron works best) over high heat. When the oil ripples in the pan, add the steaks and cook until each side is well browned, about 45 seconds per side. Sear the edges by holding the steaks on their sides with tongs until browned.

Slice the steaks on the bias to your desired thickness. Spoon the reduction onto the middle of the plate and arrange the sliced steak on top. Garnish with pickled onions and finishing salt.

NOTE: To cook the steaks sous vide, place 1 to 2 steaks in each food-grade plastic bag (depending on size) and vacuum seal each bag. Set your sous vide wand in a pot of water (you could also bring a pot of water to a boil over the stovetop with a thermometer in it) and bring the water to your desired temperature (I prefer 130°F for New York steaks). Cook the steaks for at least 1 hour at that temperature. If you forget to take them out at the 1-hour mark, you won't necessarily have done any damage. The beauty of sous vide is that you're cooking to a designated internal temperature.

Many of the great classic dishes of Belgian cuisine are well-known on American shores but assumed to be French. Americans may have heard the culinary term *carbonnade* and assumed it was French. When they think of beef and booze stews it's probably *boeuf bourguignon* (a French beef and wine dish) they think of, not the classic Belgian beef and beer stew, the carbonnade.

The key to a great carbonnade, surprisingly, isn't the beef or the beer but rather the slow caramelization of the onions. That process brings out the incredible inherent sweetness of the onions, which then combines with the beer and beef stock to create a dish that is an umami bomb.

The biggest problem with the classic dish is that it, like many meat stews, isn't exactly what your grandmother might have called "a looker." It's brown. It's homely. But the orange carrots, purple potatoes, and pink pickled onions of this version make it nearly as good to look at as it is to taste.

BEEF CARBONNADE WITH CARROTS, PURPLE POTATOES, AND PINK PICKLED ONIONS

SERVES 4 TO 6

2 pounds beef chuck, trimmed and cut into 1-inch chunks

Salt and freshly ground black pepper

3 tablespoons grapeseed, canola, or another neutral oil

4 large yellow onions, thinly sliced

1 tablespoon tomato paste

3 cloves garlic, chopped

¼ cup all-purpose flour

1 cup dark Belgian-style ale

1 cup Chicken Stock (page 151)

1 cup Beef Stock (page 152)

2 tablespoons apple cider vinegar

4 sprigs thyme

2 bay leaves

½ pound baby purple potatoes, halved lengthwise

½ pound small or baby carrots, peeled

Preheat the oven to 300°F.

Season the beef with salt and pepper. In a Dutch oven or other oven-safe pot, heat 2 tablespoons of the oil over medium-high heat. Brown the beef in batches to avoid crowding the pan, about 8 minutes per batch. When all the pieces are nicely caramelized, transfer to a plate and set aside.

Add the remaining 1 tablespoon oil to the pot, turn the heat down to medium-low, stir in the onions, and season with salt. Cook until they just begin to brown, about 8 minutes, then turn the heat up to medium and cook until the onions are fully golden, about 14 to 15 minutes. Add the tomato paste, garlic, and flour, stir, and cook for 2 minutes to combine. Add the ale and deglaze the pot by scraping the bits of fond off the bottom of the pot.

Add the chicken and beef stocks, vinegar, thyme sprigs, and bay leaves along with the cooked meat with its juices and bring to a boil. Reduce the heat to maintain a low simmer, partly cover the pot, and simmer the stew for 2½ hours.

2 tablespoons extra-virgin olive oil

1 tablespoon chopped fresh rosemary

1 tablespoon chopped fresh thyme

2 tablespoons chopped fresh parsley

Pink Pickled Onions (page 177)

Preheat the oven to 425°F and line a baking sheet with parchment paper.

About 2 hours into the cooking time, toss the potatoes and carrots with the olive oil, rosemary, and thyme on the prepared baking sheet and season with salt and pepper. Transfer to the oven and roast for 30 minutes, or until the tip of a knife goes halfway into the potatoes without much effort, stirring halfway through. Top with one tablespoon of the parsley.

When the stew is done, remove the thyme and bay leaves. Arrange the carrots and potatoes on one side of wide, shallow bowls and ladle the stew in the center of the bowl. Garnish with the remaining parsley and the pickled onions.

NOTE: All unflavored beers from Belgium, Canada, England, Germany, Mexico, Norway, and the Netherlands are kosher.

PANTRY

STOCKS

Stocks are the foundation of many elements of cuisine. They're the basis of classic sauces, soups, and stews, and they provide a solid base for just about any dish. Matching proteins—chicken stock for a chicken dish, for example—makes sense but is, ultimately, a matter of taste. Mix and match for different effects. While a beef stock might be the classic to use for a sauce to go with steak, mushroom stock could add a whole new dimension.

Follow the recipes as desired for the described result. But use what you have. You can also make a great stock in large part through the frugal use of vegetable trimmings. That's exactly what's done in many professional kitchens (and kosher households).

CHICKEN STOCK

MAKES ABOUT 3 QUARTS

Extra-virgin olive oil

5 pounds chicken bones (such as backs, wings, legs, pretty much whatever you can get)

1 medium onion, roughly chopped

1 medium carrot, roughly chopped

1 large (or 2 small) ribs celery, roughly chopped

2 medium cloves garlic, peeled and crushed

2 sprigs thyme

1 bunch parsley

2 tablespoons tomato paste

4 quarts water

2 tablespoons salt

Preheat the oven to 400°F with a rack set in the middle position and bring a small saucepan of water to a boil.

Drizzle olive oil over all the chicken parts and arrange in an even layer in a roasting pan. Transfer to the oven and roast, turning once or twice, until the bones turn golden brown, about 30 minutes. Transfer the roasted chicken bones to a stockpot.

Pour off and discard (or save) any accumulated fat from the roasting pan. Pour a little boiling water into the roasting pan and scrape up any browned bits with a wooden spoon or spatula. Add the browned bits and juices to the stockpot.

Add the onion, carrot, celery, garlic, thyme, parsley, tomato paste, 4 quarts water, and salt to the stockpot and bring to a boil over high heat. Reduce the heat to maintain a very gentle simmer and cook, uncovered, for about 1½ hours, until the stock takes on a pronounced chicken flavor, skimming off the foam periodically. Pour the stock through a fine-mesh strainer, discarding the solids. Let the stock cool to room temperature, then transfer to containers and refrigerate until completely chilled, about 6 hours. Skim off and remove any fat and scum on the surface before using. Refrigerate for up to 5 days or freeze for up to 6 months.

BEEF STOCK

MAKES ABOUT 3 QUARTS

Extra-virgin olive oil

5 pounds beef bones (such as neck, legs, or pretty much anything you can get from your butcher)

1 medium onion, roughly chopped

1 medium carrot, roughly chopped

1 large (or 2 small) ribs celery, roughly chopped

2 medium cloves garlic, peeled and crushed

2 sprigs thyme

1 sprig parsley

2 tablespoons tomato paste

4 quarts water

2 tablespoons salt

Preheat the oven to 400°F with a rack set in the middle position and bring a small saucepan of water to a boil.

Drizzle olive oil over the beef bones and arrange in an even layer in a roasting pan. Transfer to the oven and roast, turning once or twice, until the bones begin to brown, about 15 minutes.

Lightly toss the onion, carrot, and celery in the oil. Scatter the vegetables around and over the bones and continue roasting until the bones and vegetables are nicely browned, about 30 minutes longer. Be careful not to let anything scorch. Monitor the bones and rotate them if the bones on one side of the pan are browning too fast. Transfer the roasted bones to a stockpot and add the onion, carrot, celery, garlic, thyme, parsley, tomato paste, 4 quarts water, and the salt.

Pour off and discard (or save) any accumulated fat from the roasting pan. Pour a little boiling water into the roasting pan and scrape up any browned bits with a wooden spoon or spatula. Add the browned bits and juices to the stockpot.

Bring the contents of the stockpot to a boil over high heat. Reduce the heat to maintain a very gentle simmer and cook, uncovered, for at least 3 hours and up to 6 hours, until it takes on a distinct beef flavor, skimming off the foam periodically. Pour the stock through a fine-mesh strainer into a heatproof bowl, discarding the solids. Let the stock let cool to room temperature, then transfer to containers and refrigerate until completely chilled, about 6 hours. Skim off and remove any fat and scum on the surface before using. Refrigerate for up to 5 days or freeze for up to 6 months.

Vegetable stocks are common in many cuisines. This is a straightforward version of one with one key addition: kombu. The purpose of including the dried kelp in the stock is that it provides a huge dose of umami. Kombu can be found in most Asian (and all Japanese) markets.

VEGETABLE STOCK

MAKES ABOUT 3 QUARTS

1 ounce dried mushrooms (shiitake, oyster, porcini, or morel)

1 medium onion, roughly chopped

1 large carrot, roughly chopped

2 large (or 4 small) ribs celery, roughly chopped

3 leeks, green parts only (reserve the whites for another use), cleaned and roughly chopped

4 cloves garlic, peeled and crushed

2 large russet potatoes, peeled and roughly chopped

1 (4-inch) piece kombu

3 bay leaves

6 sprigs thyme

6 sprigs parsley

1 tablespoon whole black peppercorns

1 tablespoon whole white peppercorns

1 teaspoon fennel seeds

1 teaspoon coriander seeds

1 tablespoon salt (plus more as needed)

Combine all ingredients in a large stockpot and add water to cover, about 4 quarts. Bring to a boil over high heat, then reduce the heat to maintain a simmer and cook, uncovered, until the vegetables lose their texture and the stock takes on a soft but distinctly vegetal flavor, about 1 hour. Strain the stock into a heatproof bowl, discarding the solids. Taste the stock and add additional salt if required. Cool the stock, uncovered, to room temperature, then cover and transfer to the refrigerator until completely chilled, about 6 hours. Refrigerate for up to 5 days or freeze for up to 6 months.

hile the Vegetable Stock (page 154) is perfect for a wide variety of applications, sometimes you want a richer, deeper, and more powerful starting point for your soup or sauce. The answer lies in roasting the vegetables.

ROASTED VEGETABLE STOCK

MAKES ABOUT 2 QUARTS

2 large onions, roughly chopped

1 leek, white and green parts, cleaned and roughly chopped

4 large carrots, cut into chunks

2 large (or 4 small) ribs celery, roughly chopped

4 large tomatoes, roughly chopped

1 medium parsnip, peeled and roughly chopped

2 medium potatoes, peeled and quartered

6 cloves garlic, peeled and crushed

20 medium white mushrooms (about ¾ pound), trimmed and halved

2 tablespoons tomato paste

⅓ cup extra-virgin olive oil

¼ cup soy sauce

10 sprigs parsley

2 or 3 sprigs thyme

10 whole black peppercorns

½ cup white wine

Salt

Preheat the oven to 400°F with a rack set in the middle position.

In a heavy-bottomed roasting pan, toss the onions, leek, carrots, celery, tomatoes, parsnip, potatoes, garlic, mushrooms, and tomato paste with the olive oil to coat. Transfer to the oven and roast, shaking occasionally and turning the ingredients once or twice, until everything is nicely browned, about 45 minutes. While the vegetables roast, bring a medium saucepan of water to a boil.

Transfer the vegetables to a large stockpot. Set the empty roasting pan across two burners and turn both to high heat. Pour in 2 cups of boiling water, scraping off all the browned bits from the bottom of the roasting pan. Pour the water and browned bits into the stockpot with the vegetables along with 2 more cups of water.

Add the soy sauce, parsley, thyme, peppercorns, wine, and salt to the stockpot along with an additional 4 cups of water. Bring to a boil, then reduce the heat to low and simmer, partially covered, until the vegetables begin to lose their texture, 30 to 45 minutes. Taste and adjust the seasonings accordingly. Strain through a fine-mesh strainer, pressing on the vegetables to force out as much stock as possible. Let cool to room temperature, then transfer the stock to containers and refrigerate until completely chilled, about 6 hours. Refrigerate for up to 5 days or freeze for up to 6 months.

MUSHROOM STOCK

MAKES ABOUT 2 QUARTS

1 ounce dried mushrooms (shiitake, oyster, porcini, or morel)

1 medium onion, roughly chopped

1 leek, white and green parts, cleaned and roughly chopped

4 cloves garlic, peeled and crushed

1 tablespoon salt

2 tablespoons extra-virgin olive oil

½ teaspoon black peppercorns

½ pound white or cremini mushrooms, sliced

1 large (or 2 small) carrots, roughly chopped

6 sprigs parsley

3 sprigs thyme

2 sprigs marjoram or oregano

2 bay leaves

In a small pot, bring 1 cup of water to a boil over high heat. Add the dried mushrooms to a bowl and pour the water over them.

In a large stockpot, sweat the onion, leek, garlic, and salt in the olive oil over low heat for 10 minutes. Transfer the rehydrated mushrooms (with their liquid) to the stockpot along with the peppercorns, sliced mushrooms, carrots, parsley, thyme, marjoram, and bay leaves and cover with 3 quarts cold water. Bring to a boil over high heat, then reduce the heat and simmer, uncovered, for 1 hour, or until the stock takes on a distinct mushroom flavor, periodically skimming and discarding the foam. Pour the stock through a fine-mesh strainer into a heatproof bowl, pressing as much liquid as you can from the vegetables, then discard the solids. Let cool, then transfer the stock to containers and refrigerate until completely chilled, about 6 hours. Refrigerate for up to 5 days or freeze for up to 6 months.

FISH STOCK

MAKES ABOUT 1 QUART

4 pounds bones and heads of lean, white-fleshed fish (such as snapper or bass) gills removed by your fishmonger

2 tablespoons salt

2 tablespoons grapeseed, canola, or another neutral oil

½ large yellow onion, diced

½ large bulb fennel, cored and diced (fronds and stalks reserved for another purpose)

1 medium leek, white and green parts, cleaned, halved lengthwise, and sliced

2 large ribs celery, diced

2 cloves garlic, peeled and crushed

1 cup dry white wine (such as sauvignon blanc)

4 cups water (plus more as needed)

4 sprigs parsley

2 sprigs tarragon

2 sprigs thyme

1 bay leaf

5 whole black peppercorns

Place the fish bones and heads in a large bowl, cover with cold water, and stir in the salt until dissolved. Soak the bones and head for 1 hour to extract as much of the blood as possible. Drain, then rinse the bones under cold running water to wash away any large areas of blood.

In a large stockpot, heat the oil over medium-high heat until shimmering and add the onion, fennel, leek, celery, and garlic. Reduce the heat to medium-low and cook, stirring, until the vegetables have softened slightly, about 4 minutes. Stir in the fish heads and bones. Stir periodically until the bones and any flesh turn from translucent to white, about 12 minutes.

Add the wine and cook, stirring, until it begins to steam, then add the 4 cups water so the liquid just barely covers the heads and bones. Add more water if necessary. Add the parsley, tarragon, thyme, bay leaf, and peppercorns.

Turn the heat up to high and bring the liquid to a bare simmer, then lower the heat so that it stays just below a simmer, with only the occasional bubble rising to the surface. Cook for 20 to 30 minutes, until the flavors meld. Using a spoon, skim off any foam that accumulates on the surface.

Strain the stock through a fine-mesh strainer into a heatproof bowl. Let cool, then transfer the stock to containers and refrigerate until completely chilled, about 6 hours. Refrigerate for up to 5 days or freeze for up to 3 months.

SAUCES AND DRESSINGS

There's a reason that *saucier* has always been one of the most prestigious positions in the classic French kitchen brigade system. A sauce can make or break a dish. Every cuisine has its own critical, classic sauces. Kosher cuisine is different only in that it draws from so many cuisines.

Given that dairy sauces can't be used with meat in kosher cooking, the creaminess of tahini sauce has a special role in today's Israeli cuisine. Its slight bitterness and sweetness makes it all the more beguiling. Tahini sauce is an essential ingredient in a number of recipes in this book, including the Fried Chickpeas with Tahini Sauce, Poached Egg, and Scallion Salt (page 42), Herbed Falafel with Beet Hummus (page 54), Holishkes of Jerusalem Mixed Grill and Jasmine Rice (page 78), Turkey Shawarma with Garlic and Herb Tahini and Pickled Red Cabbage (page 82), and Coffee Braised Lamb Shoulder in Pita (page 81).

TAHINI SAUCE
MAKES ABOUT 2 CUPS

1 cup tahini paste

¼ cup fresh lemon juice (plus more as needed)

2 small cloves garlic, minced

Salt

1 cup water

1 tablespoon ground sumac, for garnish (optional)

Combine the tahini paste, lemon juice, and garlic in the bowl of a food processor and process to combine, about 20 seconds. With the machine running, add ¾ cup water in a steady stream through the feed tube to form a smooth, creamy mixture approximately the thickness of heavy cream, about another 30 seconds. Taste the sauce and adjust the balance of water, salt, and lemon juice as preferred. Turn the tahini sauce out into a bowl and garnish with the sumac, if desired. The sauce keeps well, properly sealed, in the refrigerator for up to 5 days.

chug is the go-to hot sauce in Israel. It came with the Yemeni Jews and ranges from merely spicy to nearly nuclear. It comes in both green and red varieties, with the commonality being the heat, the garlic, and the herbal element. In Israel schug is a natural accompaniment for shawarma, falafel, or Jerusalem mixed grills based on the cuisines of origin but could be used happily anywhere that any hot sauce works. Choose green or red schug to match the color or flavor of the dish with which you're pairing it.

GREEN SCHUG

YIELDS ABOUT 1½ CUPS

1 large bunch cilantro (leaves and tender stems)

1 head garlic (about 12 cloves)

3 large (about 1 ounce each) hot green chiles (such as jalapeño or serrano)

1 teaspoon salt

1 teaspoon freshly ground black pepper

3 tablespoons extra-virgin olive oil (plus more for storing)

1 tablespoon fresh lemon juice

Rinse and dry and coarsely chop the cilantro. Peel and chop the garlic.

Combine the cilantro, garlic, and chiles in the bowl of a food processor, pulse several times, then process it to a chunky paste, about 20 seconds. Add the salt and pepper and pulse to incorporate.

With the processor running, stream the olive oil through the feed tube in a steady stream to incorporate. Transfer to a bowl or container and stir in the lemon juice (this will preserve the color). Cover the surface with olive oil, cover, and store in the refrigerator for 4 to 5 days.

RED
SCHUG

GREEN
SCHUG

The character of the schug, whether red or green, is based primarily on the choice of specific chiles used in the sauce (as well as the color). Feel free to experiment with different chiles at different heat levels.

RED SCHUG

YIELDS ABOUT 1½ CUPS

½ large bunch cilantro (leaves and tender stems)

1 head garlic (about 12 cloves)

6 large (about 1 ounce each) hot red chiles (such as Fresnos)

1 teaspoon salt

1 teaspoon freshly ground black pepper

3 tablespoons extra-virgin olive oil (plus more for storing)

1 tablespoon fresh lemon juice

Rinse and dry and coarsely chop the cilantro. Peel and chop the garlic.

Combine the cilantro, garlic, and chiles in the bowl of a food processor, pulse several times, then process to a chunky paste, about 20 seconds. Add the salt and pepper and pulse to incorporate.

With the processor running, stream the olive oil through the feed tube in a steady stream to incorporate. Transfer to a bowl or container and stir in the lemon juice (this will preserve the color). Cover the surface with olive oil, cover, and store in the refrigerator for 4 to 5 days.

himichurri sauce is the natural mate to good-quality meat; and, in this book I use it as just that in the Empanadas of Minced Beef, Olives, and Capers with Chimichurri (page 113). In Argentina, however, it's used in larger, different formats. In that spirit, it is an excellent way to jazz up a perfectly grilled steak on a summer weekend afternoon.

The key to chimichurri's versatility lies in the combination of fresh herbs, heat from the chiles, funk from the garlic, and acidity from the vinegar along with the richness from the oil.

CHIMICHURRI SAUCE

MAKES ABOUT 2 CUPS

½ cup firmly packed fresh parsley leaves

½ cup firmly packed fresh cilantro leaves and stems (the stems are where the flavor is)

3 to 4 (depending on heat) jalapeño chiles, stemmed, seeded, and chopped

3 cloves garlic, peeled

¼ cup red wine vinegar

1 teaspoon salt

¼ teaspoon freshly ground black pepper

¾ cup extra-virgin olive oil

In the bowl of a food processor or blender, combine the parsley, cilantro, jalapeños, garlic, vinegar, salt, and pepper. Pulse to break down large pieces, then process on low speed to combine, and, finally, increase the speed to high and drizzle in the oil through the feed tube in a steady stream until fully incorporated and puréed. Check the seasoning for balance and adjust to taste. Cover and chill for at least 3 hours. Store covered in the refrigerator for up to 3 days.

Those speaking English in India (and Britain) use the word "coriander" for what we Americans call "cilantro" (though we do call the spice made from grinding the seeds of the same plant "coriander"). We are, after all, divided by a common language. Coriander chutney is a condiment that borders on the ubiquitous on the Indian table, ranging from not remotely spicy to "nuclear," depending on the chile pepper quotient.

CORIANDER (CILANTRO) CHUTNEY

MAKES ABOUT 2 CUPS

1 large bunch cilantro (about 2 ounces), roughly chopped

6 scallions (green parts only; whites reserved for another purpose), coarsely chopped

2 hot green chiles (such as serrano or Thai bird), roughly chopped

1 teaspoon sugar

2 tablespoons peeled and chopped fresh ginger

1 teaspoon ground cumin

¼ cup fresh lemon juice

1 teaspoon salt

¼ cup extra-virgin olive oil

In a blender, combine the cilantro, scallions, chiles, sugar, ginger, cumin, lemon juice, and salt. Blend at medium speed, slowly drizzling in the olive oil through the feed tube, until smooth, about 20 seconds. Store refrigerated in an airtight container for up to 3 days.

Amba is Urdu (the Persian version of Hindi) for mango, and the sauce is Israel's unique take on the classic Indian theme of mango chutney. This Israeli version of the sauce is sour, sweet, salty, and rich with a more garlic forward flavor profile.

Israeli chefs pair amba with just about anything, especially (if not exclusively) if it goes in pita. In this book it appears in the Pickled Halibut with Persian Cucumbers, Amba Sauce, and Horseradish Cream (page 44) and Holishkes of Jerusalem Mixed Grill and Jasmine Rice (page 78).

For my version I use one ripe mango and one unripe mango. The ripe mango contributes sweetness and the unripe mango offers a tangy zing.

AMBA (PICKLED MANGO) SAUCE

MAKES ABOUT 1½ CUPS

1 ripe mango and 1 unripe mango (about 1½ pounds total)

2 large lemons

1½ tablespoons extra-virgin olive oil

2 cloves garlic, minced

½ teaspoon yellow mustard seeds

½ teaspoon fenugreek seeds

½ teaspoon Aleppo pepper

½ teaspoon Spanish smoked paprika (pimenton)

½ teaspoon ground turmeric

½ teaspoon ground cumin

Peel the mangos, cut the flesh of the fruit from the pit, and add it to the bowl of a food processor. Zest the lemons with a grater, reserving the fruit, and add the zest to the food processor. Pulse several times to combine, then increase the speed and process to purée, about 20 seconds.

Heat the olive oil in a small sauté pan over medium heat. When hot, add the garlic, mustard seeds, fenugreek seeds, Aleppo pepper, smoked paprika, turmeric, and cumin and cook until the garlic is lightly golden, shaking the pan occasionally, about 2 to 3 minutes. Add the puréed mango to the pan and stir to combine. Taste and adjust the seasoning by adding salt or lemon juice, as desired. Let the sauce cool, then cover, transfer to the refrigerator, and store for up to 1 week.

AMBA
SAUCE

SOFREGIT

CORIANDER
CHUTNEY

discovered *sofregit* on a trip to Barcelona. It shares a common origin and is almost identical to the *sofritos* of the rest of Spain (as well as Italy and much of Latin America), but contemporary Spanish versions often use green bell peppers rather than red. Sofregit's most common use in Catalan cuisine is as a marvelous flavor base for soups, sauces, and many other recipes. Take just about any recipe that uses a classic French mirepoix (onion, celery, carrot) or the Cajun "Holy Trinity" (onion, celery, and green pepper) and swap those out in favor of a sofregit—which melds as it cooks into a single flavor profile that's both savory and sweet—and you immediately give the dish a Catalan personality.

Sofregit can also function as a finishing element in its own right; for example, wherever you might use tomato confit, because both feature the wonderfully intense umami flavors from the tomato.

SOFREGIT

MAKES ABOUT 1½ CUPS

1 pound (about 8) medium tomatoes

¼ cup extra-virgin olive oil

2 medium onions, finely chopped

1 red bell pepper, finely chopped

½ teaspoon sugar (optional)

Bring a medium pot of water to a boil over high heat and prepare an ice bath. Make a small (⅛ inch) X-shaped incision on the very blossom end of each tomato, opposite the stem. Carefully add the tomatoes to the pot and blanch for 10 seconds (do this in batches if you need to), then remove and plunge immediately into the ice bath to stop the cooking. Once the tomatoes are cooled enough to handle, starting from the X-shaped incision, use your hands or a paring knife to strip the skins from the blanched tomatoes, then dice.

Heat the olive oil in heavy-bottomed soup pot or Dutch oven over high heat until it shimmers. Add the onions and cook for 2 minutes. Add the bell pepper, stir, and cook until the onions just begin to caramelize, 10 to 12 minutes, stirring often with a wooden spoon.

Add the chopped tomatoes and stir to combine. If the tomatoes are not particularly sweet, stir in the sugar. Cover and cook, stirring occasionally, until the vegetables lose their texture, 15 to 30 minutes.

Cool completely, then transfer to an airtight storage container and cover with a thin layer of olive oil. Store in the refrigerator for up to 3 weeks.

There are many decent mayonnaise products in nearly every grocery store in America. Some even say that Hellmann's or Best Foods brand (depending on where you are) is the best mayo on the rock. They're wrong. Perhaps it's the best store-bought mayo (though I'd argue that the Japanese Kewpie brand is far better). But the best altogether? Not in my totally non-humble opinion.

Anyone with a food processor or blender can make a better mayo with ease. Start with good-quality fresh ingredients and be sure to use a neutral oil. If you want to take the finished product further in the direction of an aioli, double or even triple the garlic. See, for example, the California Fisherman's Cioppino (page 125).

MAYONNAISE

MAKES ABOUT 1½ CUPS

1 clove garlic, peeled and crushed

1 teaspoon salt

1 large egg plus 1 additional yolk

1 tablespoon Dijon mustard

Juice of 1 lemon

1½ cups grapeseed, canola, or another neutral oil

Place the garlic and salt in the bowl of a food processor. Pulse until the garlic is pulverized, 4 or 5 times. Add the egg and yolk to the bowl and process until fully integrated, about 5 seconds. Add the mustard and lemon juice and process to fully combine, another 5 to 10 seconds. With the machine running, slowly drizzle in the oil through the feed tube, almost drop by drop, until it is fully incorporated and the sauce is emulsified and smooth. Store in an airtight container in the refrigerator for up to a week.

Garum is a magical, delicious potion that was the go-to flavor-enhancing condiment of ancient Rome. The closest analog today would be the fermented fish sauces of Southeast Asia. Recently, Western cuisine seems to have rediscovered the wonders of garum, with high-end chefs, including Noma's René Redzepi and State Bird Provisions' Stuart Brioza, producing home-brewed versions. This recipe follows Brioza's lead, using some different flavoring ingredients. Feel free to experiment with the spices to adjust the flavor profile in whatever direction you want to take it.

Like fish sauce, garum is one of those umami-intense ingredients that, when used in moderation, makes everything around it taste better. It reveals flavor dimensions you did not know were in there! I've used it in this book in the Quick Tomato Sauce (page 173) and suggested it as an addition to the Lasagnette of Mushrooms, House-Made Ricotta, and Mint-Pepita Pesto (page 123), but you could add it to just about any sauce (or, for that matter, any savory dish) and it will make the dish better and cure what ails you.

GARUM

MAKES ABOUT 2½ CUPS

2 cups fish sauce

½ cup fresh lime juice

1-inch segment from the inner white section of a lemongrass stalk

1-inch knob of fresh ginger, peeled and roughly chopped

2 whole cloves

1 whole star anise

¼ teaspoon coriander seeds

¼ teaspoon fenugreek seeds

1 whole cardamom pod

In the bowl of a high-speed blender or food processor, combine the fish sauce, lime juice, lemongrass, ginger, cloves, star anise, coriander, fenugreek, and cardamom pod. Starting at the lowest speed (or, if using a food processor, by pulsing), break up the solids and process to combine all of the ingredients. Gradually increase the speed and process on high speed until mixture is nearly puréed, about 1 minute.

Transfer the mixture to a pickling jar or other airtight container and refrigerate for at least 24 hours and up to 1 month. The longer it sits, the more the fish sauce will be infused with the flavors of the spices. Strain the sauce through a fine-mesh strainer and discard the solids. The garum will keep for up to 3 months in the refrigerator.

NOTE: To prep the lemongrass for this recipe, trim off the outer layer, spiky tops, and bases. Carefully crush the stalks with the flat side of a chef's knife to release the aromatic oils, then chop into 1-inch pieces.

This is the classic salsa served with chips throughout the United States. Truly a Mexican salsa, it's called *salsa bandera* because it features the colors of the Mexican flag (*bandera* translates to "flag" in Spanish). That said, you won't find it on tables in Mexico because Mexico doesn't do tortilla chips and salsa; that's an American thing.

The very characteristics that made salsa so popular make it a remarkably versatile sauce and condiment for the kosher cook. It could be added to absolutely any recipe in this book that is served in or with pita to give the dish a wonderfully fresh element. If Red or Green Schug (pages 162 and 160) are too spicy for you, this relatively mild salsa, also called *salsa fresca*, *salsa Mexicana*, or *pico de gallo*, makes a great substitute.

SALSA BANDERA

MAKES ABOUT 1½ CUPS

½ medium white onion, finely diced

1 pound Roma tomatoes (about 4), diced

2 jalapeño chiles, seeded and minced

3 tablespoons finely chopped fresh cilantro

2 tablespoons fresh lime juice (plus more as needed)

½ teaspoon salt (plus more as needed)

Combine the onion, tomatoes, jalapeños, cilantro, lime juice, and salt in a large bowl and mix thoroughly. Taste the salsa and adjust the seasoning by adding more salt or lime juice if necessary. Store in an airtight container in the refrigerator for up to 3 days.

SALSA
BANDERA

ROASTED
TOMATO,
ARBOL CHILE,
AND GARLIC
SLASA

The key to this salsa is toasting the chiles without burning them. While both this and the *salsa bandera* (see page 170) are Mexican-style salsas, they could hardly be more different. This recipe is a cooked salsa full of deep, intense flavors; the latter is uncooked—simple, bright, and direct.

It may seem counterintuitive to cut the tomatoes before toasting them, but to my surprise I was not getting the concentrated tomato flavor I wanted using the more traditional approach. By getting the pan smoking hot and increasing contact between the insides of the tomato and the pan, caramelizing more of the tomato's natural sugars, I achieved much better results.

ROASTED TOMATO, ARBOL CHILE, AND GARLIC SALSA

MAKES ABOUT 2 CUPS

2 Roma tomatoes

8 dried árbol chiles

4 cloves garlic, unpeeled

½ medium white onion, chopped

½ cup chopped fresh cilantro

1 teaspoon salt (plus more as needed)

Juice of 1 lime (optional)

Slice the tomatoes in half lengthwise and then slice the halves again widthwise. Heat a dry sauté pan over high heat until you can barely hold your hand an inch or two above the surface and place the tomatoes on the pan. Toast the tomatoes until their cut surface blackens on the bottom, about 2 to 3 minutes, then flip and repeat until all cut surfaces are blackened. Remove the tomatoes to the bowl of a food processor.

Toast the chiles in a large dry sauté pan over medium heat, shaking the pan occasionally, until they darken and start to brown in spots, about 2 minutes, then transfer to a small heatproof bowl. Pour ½ cup boiling water over the chiles, then cover with plastic wrap and let soak for 15 minutes. In the same sauté pan over medium heat, toast the garlic, turning regularly, until the cloves are soft and start to brown in spots, about 5 minutes. Remove from the heat and, once cooled, peel and chop the garlic. Add the chopped onion to the pan and fry until the onion is slightly caramelized, about 2 to 3 minutes.

In a food processor or blender, combine the tomatoes, chiles, chopped garlic, onions, cilantro, and salt. Pulse to combine, then process on low speed, gradually increasing to evenly chop and combine the ingredients but not purée them, about 1 minute. Taste the sauce for seasoning and add some more salt or some lime juice, if necessary. Transfer to a sealed container and refrigerate for up to a week.

A traditional Italian marinara sauce is a long, slow-cooked affair. Flavors are built up by dint of love, care, and time. This recipe is a quick and surprisingly easy, no-less satisfying substitute. Its secret is the garum (see page 169), soy sauce, and monosodium glutamate, a.k.a. "MSG" (I'm a fan of the stuff when used in moderation, but you do not have to use it if you believe the haters) as intense flavor builders and enhancers.

QUICK TOMATO SAUCE

MAKES ABOUT 4 CUPS

1 medium onion, finely chopped

1 bulb fennel, cored and finely chopped (fronds and stalks reserved for another purpose)

1 large carrot, finely chopped

1 tablespoon extra-virgin olive oil

1 (28-ounce) can whole San Marzano-style tomatoes

2 tablespoons Garum (page 169; or 2 tablespoons of fish sauce or 2 anchovies, rinsed and minced)

1 teaspoon soy sauce

1 pinch salt

1 teaspoon MSG (optional)

Red wine vinegar (optional)

Sweat the onion, fennel, and carrot in the olive oil in a large saucepan over low heat until they give up their liquid, about 2 to 3 minutes. Using your hands, crush the tomatoes, then stir them and their juices into the pot along with the garum, soy sauce, salt, and MSG (if using), then turn up the heat and bring to a boil. Reduce the heat to maintain a simmer and cook, stirring occasionally, until thickened and the surface oil achieves a deep orange color, about 15 minutes. Taste and adjust the seasonings with salt or a splash of vinegar. Depending on the texture you want, you can purée it in a high-speed blender or food processor (or not). Transfer to a sealed container in the refrigerator for no more than 4 to 5 days.

've always loved ranch, the all-American salad dressing of dried herbs and spices, buttermilk, and mayonnaise. It's creamy, with savory elements as well as sweetness and hints of sour and pungency. The best versions resemble this. Unfortunately, too many overly sweet commercial products going by the "ranch" name have turned it into a pop culture joke. That's reason enough to make your own.

But as much as I like good ranch, I couldn't help think that the fresh herbs of green goddess dressing would improve things. This recipe is a cross between the two, featuring fresh herbs as well as the buttermilk and dried spices. Thicken this recipe with a teaspoon or so (start with a half teaspoon and add more if necessary) of xanthan gum to make an excellent dip.

FRESH HERB RANCH DRESSING

MAKES ABOUT 1½ CUPS

1 cup chopped fresh dill

1 cup chopped fresh parsley

¾ cup chopped fresh chives

2 cloves garlic, peeled

½ cup plain Greek yogurt

½ cup buttermilk

¼ cup Mayonnaise (page 168)

1 teaspoon garlic powder

1 teaspoon onion powder

½ teaspoon freshly ground black pepper

½ teaspoon freshly ground white pepper

2 teaspoons fresh lemon juice

1 teaspoon Texas Pete's (or other Louisiana-style) hot sauce

1 teaspoon salt

In the bowl of a high-speed blender or food processor, combine the dill, parsley, chives, garlic, yogurt, buttermilk, mayonnaise, garlic powder, onion powder, black pepper, white pepper, lemon juice, hot sauce, and salt. Starting on low speed and then increasing to high, process to purée, about 1 minute, stopping to scrape down the sides of the bowl from time to time. Taste and adjust the seasonings if necessary. Chill until ready to serve and store in an airtight container in the refrigerator for up to 3 to 5 days.

For my fortieth birthday, my wife and I, along with friends who are much better sailors than we, took a sailboat from Athens out via the Corinth Canal up the west coast of Greece to Corfu. At every port there was a *taverna* (or ten) serving Greek salads featuring a dressing a lot like this one.

It remains, to this day, my go-to salad dressing for any just about any green salad. The key to what makes it so good is the combination of the two acids—the sweetness of the red wine vinegar coupled with the fruitiness of the lemon juice.

For something different to do with this dressing, try using it as a marinade for chicken. It's an excellent base for other preparations, which is exactly how I use it in the Grilled Leeks with Asparagus Vinaigrette (page 60) and Tuna-Stuffed Tomatoes with Fresh Dill Vinaigrette (page 102).

LEMON AND RED WINE VINAIGRETTE

MAKES ABOUT ¾ CUP

2 tablespoons red wine vinegar

2 tablespoons fresh lemon juice

1 clove garlic, minced

½ teaspoon dried oregano

½ teaspoon salt

¼ teaspoon freshly ground black pepper

½ cup extra-virgin olive oil

In a large bowl, combine the vinegar, lemon juice, garlic, oregano, salt, pepper, and olive oil and whisk vigorously to combine. Chill until ready to serve and store in an airtight container in the refrigerator for up to 1 week. Allow the refrigerated dressing to come to room temperature and mix well before using.

PICKLES

One of the best ways to add a new dimension to any dish is by tossing in a pickle. The first thought many people have when they hear that word when accompanied by the idea of doing it themselves is *"How long* will it take?" When it comes to pickles, the answer is not very long at all.

These are quick pickles. They're not the time- and space-consuming dill or half-sour pickles our grandparents put up by the quart. They're done in under an hour, not in a matter of days. You could get home from work and have them done in time for dinner. Quick pickles, frankly, are one of the cook's best tools—maybe even "cheats"—to elevate any dish quickly and easily. Pickled cabbage is an excellent (and brilliantly colorful) addition to any taco or pita dish. Pickled onions do that same trick well and work great on any slab of meat.

I am, frankly, passionate about pickles. They're well represented in this book, including in the following dishes: the pickled garlic in the Tomato Matzo Ball Soup with Pickled Garlic Chives (page 27), the pickled serrano chiles in Pho Ga with Matzo Noodles (page 30), the pickled blackberries on the Latkes with Smoked Salmon, Pickled Blackberry, and Wasabi Cream (page 33), and pickled onions on numerous dishes including the Chopped Chicken Liver Montadito with Pickled Onions and Radish Sprouts (page 32).

PICKLED RED CABBAGE

MAKES ABOUT 1 QUART

1½ pounds red cabbage (about ½ small head), thinly sliced

2 cloves garlic, crushed

6 dried árbol chiles

6 allspice berries

12 coriander seeds

½ cup red wine vinegar

½ cup apple cider vinegar

2 tablespoons brown sugar

Place the cabbage in a large heatproof bowl. Combine the garlic, chiles, allspice, coriander seeds, red wine vinegar, cider vinegar, brown sugar, and 1 cup water in a medium pot and bring to boil over high heat. Pour the mixture over the cabbage and stir. Let cool to room temperature, then transfer to the refrigerator to chill for at least 1 hour. The pickles will keep refrigerated in a sealed container for up to 1 week.

PINK PICKLED ONIONS

MAKES ABOUT 1 QUART

2 red onions, halved and thinly sliced

1 cup red wine vinegar

½ cup sugar

6 allspice berries

20 black peppercorns

¼ cup salt

1 bay leaf

Place the onions in a bowl and cover with boiling water. Let stand for 1 minute, then drain. Combine the vinegar, sugar, allspice, peppercorns, salt, bay leaf, and 1 cup water in a small saucepan and bring to a boil over high heat. Pour over the onions and let stand for 1 to 2 hours. The pickles will keep refrigerated in a sealed container for up to 2 weeks.

PICKLED SHALLOTS

MAKES ABOUT 2 CUPS

8 shallots, thinly sliced (about ⅓ cup total)

2 teaspoons whole coriander seeds, coarsely crushed

½ cup apple cider vinegar

½ cup red wine vinegar

1 tablespoon light brown sugar

2 teaspoons salt

Place the shallots in a glass quart jar. Sprinkle the coriander seeds over the top. Combine the cider vinegar, red wine vinegar, brown sugar, and salt in a small nonreactive saucepan and bring to a boil over medium heat, stirring to dissolve the sugar and salt.

Pour the brine over the shallots and let stand for 1 to 2 hours until cool before sealing the jar. Chill in the refrigerator at least 1 day before using. The pickles will keep refrigerated in a sealed container for up to 2 weeks.

PICKLED SCALLIONS

MAKES ABOUT 1 QUART

2 bunches scallions, cut in half crosswise and both ends trimmed

2 tablespoons finely chopped fresh tarragon leaves

1 tablespoon yellow mustard seeds

2 teaspoons coriander seeds

1 teaspoon cumin seeds

2 cups white wine vinegar

1 cup sugar

2 tablespoons salt

Pack the scallions and tarragon into a glass quart jar. Toast the mustard, coriander, and cumin seeds in a small dry saucepan over medium-low heat, tossing often, until fragrant, about 2 minutes. Add to the jar.

In the same saucepan, bring the vinegar, sugar, and salt to a simmer over medium heat, stirring to dissolve the sugar and salt. Pour the brine over the scallions and seal the jar. Chill in the refrigerator at least 1 day before using. The pickles will keep refrigerated in a sealed container for up to 1 week.

PICKLED SERRANO CHILES

MAKES ABOUT 2 CUPS

2 cups whole serrano chiles, thinly sliced into very fine rings (about ⅛ inch)

1½ cups distilled vinegar

3 cloves garlic, peeled

2 tablespoons black peppercorns

2 tablespoons sugar

2 tablespoons coriander seeds

2 tablespoons salt

Pack the chiles into a sanitized 1-quart jar. Combine the vinegar, garlic, peppercorns, sugar, coriander seeds, salt, and 1½ cups water in a medium saucepan and bring to a boil over high heat. Reduce the heat to medium and simmer for 5 minutes. Pour the hot brine over the chiles in the jar and set aside to cool. Seal the jar and transfer to the refrigerator. Once cooled the pickles are ready to eat. They will keep refrigerated in a sealed container for up to 1 month.

QUICK PRESERVED LEMONS

MAKES ABOUT ¼ CUP

3 or 4 large lemons

1 tablespoon salt

With a very sharp knife, slice the biggest and prettiest lemon crosswise into ¼-inch-thick rounds and gently remove the seeds. Juice the other lemons to yield ½ cup fresh lemon juice.

Combine the lemon slices, juice, and salt in a medium saucepan. Bring to a boil over high heat, stirring to dissolve the salt. Cover, reduce the heat to low, and simmer until the lemon slices are almost tender and the peel looks translucent, about 10 minutes. Transfer the lemon slices and brine to a glass container and set aside to cool. Once cooled, transfer to the refrigerator, where they will keep for up to 1 week.

use these in the Latkes with Smoked Salmon, Pickled Blackberry, and Wasabi Cream (page 33), but they would be excellent in a salad, on a morning bagel, or as a garnish (or even in a sauce) for meats. In fact, the same basic techniques in this recipe would work equally well for other berries, like raspberries or blueberries.

PICKLED BLACKBERRIES

MAKES ABOUT 1 QUART

10 whole black peppercorns

2 allspice berries

2 juniper berries

1 dried árbol chile, stemmed

1-inch piece fresh ginger, peeled and thinly sliced

1 bay leaf

6 tablespoons sugar

3 tablespoons salt

2 cups apple cider vinegar

1 shallot, thinly sliced horizontally

1 sprig thyme

1 pound blackberries (about 3¼ cups)

Using a mortar and pestle, lightly crush the peppercorns, allspice berries, juniper berries, chile, ginger, and bay leaf. Combine the crushed spices with the sugar and salt in a large bowl and add the vinegar and 2 cups of water. Whisk to combine. Transfer to a medium saucepan, add the shallots and thyme, and bring just to a boil over high heat, stirring to make sure the solids are fully dissolved. Transfer back to the bowl and let cool completely.

Add the blackberries to a sanitized 1-quart glass jar. Strain the brine and pour it over the berries to cover. Cover and refrigerate for at least 1 week before serving. The pickled blackberries will keep, refrigerated, for up to 3 months.

PICKLED
RED
CABBAGE

PICKLED
BLACK
BERRIES

QUICK
PRESERVED
LEMONS,
CENTER

PICKLED
ONIONS

HERB AND SPICE BLENDS

The spice blends imported by Sephardic Jews back to Israel from their former homes across North Africa and the Middle East have become cornerstones of New Israeli cuisine. Two popular spice blends go by the names *baharat* and *ras el hanout*, and while these names sound exotic and very specific, *baharat* simply translates as "spices" and *ras el hanout* as "top of the shelf," suggesting the precise blend of spices can vary from family to family by taste, as in Indian curries or Mexican moles. They can be and often are used in many ways beyond the specific dishes in this book—one of the best is to combine them with olive oil and lemon juice as a marinade for meat.

All of the spice blends can be stored in an airtight jar in the pantry for two to three weeks. They won't exactly "go bad," but their potency drops off steadily.

Dried herb powders have the power to utterly transform a dish. The recipes here should be just a start. The salted ash from Beet and Potato Latkes with Crème Fraîche, Chopped Chives, and Salted Ash (page 36) and the fenugreek salt from Beet Tartare with Greek Yogurt, Capers, and Fenugreek Salt (page 92) could easily fit in this section.

POULTRY SHAWARMA SPICE BLEND

MAKES ABOUT 1½ CUPS

½ cup ground turmeric

½ cup ground cumin

2 tablespoons freshly ground black pepper

2 tablespoons freshly ground white pepper

2 tablespoons ground cardamom

2 teaspoons ground coriander

1 teaspoon ground cinnamon

2 tablespoons salt

Combine all the ingredients in a small bowl and mix together.

RED MEAT SHAWARMA SPICE BLEND

MAKES ABOUT 1½ CUPS

½ cup ground sumac

¼ cup smoked paprika

2 tablespoons freshly ground black pepper

2 tablespoons garlic powder

2 tablespoons onion powder

1 tablespoon Aleppo pepper (or cayenne pepper)

1 tablespoon ground cardamom

2 teaspoons salt

Combine all the ingredients in a small bowl and mix well.

BAHARAT SPICE BLEND

MAKES ABOUT ½ CUP

2 tablespoons freshly ground black pepper

1 tablespoon freshly grated nutmeg

1 tablespoon paprika

2 teaspoons ground coriander

2 teaspoons ground cinnamon

2 teaspoons ground cloves

2 teaspoons ground cumin

½ teaspoon ground cardamom

2 teaspoons salt

Combine all the ingredients in a small bowl and mix well.

Herb salts can work wonders on a dish. In fact, get creative and an herb salt can serve at least half the function of a sauce. A light dusting and you add a whole new dimension to a dish.

This recipe can be adapted to any soft herb or combination of herbs. Add parsley and celery greens along with the scallion greens here and you have a wonderful blend for steamed fish. Poached eggs have become something of a cliché in contemporary cuisine, but a sprinkling of this scallion salt—as in Fried Chickpeas with Tahini Sauce, Poached Egg, and Scallion Salt (page 42)—adds a new dimension to the dish. Examples of similar blends include the salted ash from the Beet and Potato Latkes on page 36 and the fenugreek salt from the Beet Tartare on page 92. Ashes and powders are particularly useful with simply cooked fish to add another dimension of earthiness or freshness or just sauce-like flavor without a heavy sauce. Or take it another step and turn freshly dried Oven-Roasted Tomatoes (page 188) into a powder as an optional garnish for Holishkes of Jerusalem Mixed Grill and Jasmine Rice (page 78) or the Empanadas of Minced Beef, Olives, and Capers with Chimichurri (page 113).

SCALLION SALT

MAKES ABOUT ⅓ CUP

½ cup scallion greens (or other soft herbs)

2 tablespoons salt

Arrange the scallion greens on a parchment paper–lined baking sheet. Gently bake on as low a temperature as your oven will go (preferably lower than 200°F). If you have a dehydrator, use that at 145°F. Bake until the scallions are completely dry, at least 45 minutes, but depending on the water content of the scallions and the temperature of the oven, it could take twice as long.

Combine the dried scallion greens and salt in the bowl of a high-speed blender (you could also use a spice grinder, working in small batches) and process to a fine powder. Unused powders can be kept almost indefinitely. While the bright color of herb powders will fade within weeks, the flavor persists and can be kept indefinitely.

SALTED
ASH

SCALLION
SALT

POULTRY
SHAWARMA
SPICE BLEND

RED MEAT
SHAWARMA
SPICE BLEND

GARNISHES, FLOURISHES, AND STAPLES

Every good cook keeps ingredients in the larder they use as "secret ingredients" to take their signature dishes to the next level. These may take many different forms. One—actually, two—of the best are made together. Schmaltz and gribenes are made together but often used separately. Schmaltz is an ever-present fat in kosher kitchen refrigerators, used almost whenever butter can't be. Gribenes can feature as they do in the Tacos of Gribenes in Salsa Verde (page 76) but are more classically used in Ashkenazi kosher kitchens (and elsewhere) as a crunchy garnish or textural element.

SCHMALTZ AND GRIBENES

MAKES ABOUT 1 CUP SCHMALTZ AND ½ CUP GRIBENES

1 pound chicken skin and fat, sliced into ¾- to 1-inch pieces (see Note)

1 teaspoon salt

1 medium onion, thickly sliced

TO MAKE THE SCHMALTZ: In a large bowl, toss the chicken skin with the salt. Transfer to a cast-iron or nonreactive stainless steel skillet and set over medium-low heat—low enough to render the fat but not crisp the skin—shaking the pan occasionally to avoid sticking. Cover the pan and cook, stirring frequently and breaking the pieces apart with a spatula. You know you're on the right track when, after about 15 minutes, the liquid fat starts to pool at the bottom of the pan. Continue cooking until the skin just starts to brown and curl at the edges, 30 to 45 minutes.

Remove the pan from the heat and let cool, then pour through a strainer (reserving the crispy chicken skin) into a container, cover, and transfer to the refrigerator. This golden liquid, the patiently rendered chicken fat, is schmaltz. It will keep in the refrigerator for up to 1 week, though some of the aromatic and flavor nuances may start to disappear before that. Frozen, schmaltz keeps for up to 1 month.

TO MAKE THE GRIBENES: Return the reserved crispy chicken skin to the pan along with the onions and 1 tablespoon of the schmaltz and set over medium heat. Cook the onions and chicken skin until the skin is browned and just starting to crisp, 30 to 45 minutes, stirring frequently. If anything starts to burn, reduce the heat to low. Remove the gribenes from the skillet with a slotted spoon to drain on paper towels. Gribenes will last, properly sealed, in the refrigerator for about 1 week.

NOTE: You can easily save a pound of chicken skin and fat by reserving the skin and fat from chicken parts you cook in other meals and keeping it in the freezer. You can also buy chicken skin and fat from your local (kosher) butcher.

un-dried tomatoes are yet another example of a really good idea that ate itself. The intense flavor and inherent deliciousness of sun-dried tomatoes made them a fad that turned into a trend that became a cliché. They also fell victim to the capitalistic tendency to dumb down products as they enter the stream of commerce. The stuff you find in the supermarket tends to end up not being very good. That's solved easily, though, by making them at home.

In the kosher kitchen, sun-dried or oven-dried tomatoes can play a critical role. Their depth of flavor and umami quality make them a very fitting substitute for cured pork products in all sorts of dishes (particularly of Spanish or Italian origin). They're delicious mixed into any grain or pasta; Abe's Eggs (page 22), for example. You can customize this recipe by adding other types of herbs, garlic, or even chile flakes.

OVEN-DRIED TOMATOES

MAKES ABOUT 2 CUPS

6 pounds plum tomatoes, halved lengthwise

¼ cup fresh oregano, rosemary, and/or thyme leaves

1 teaspoon salt

1 teaspoon freshly ground black pepper

1½ cups extra-virgin olive oil (optional), for storing

Preheat the oven to 250°F and set two racks in the upper- and lower-middle of the oven. Line two baking sheets with parchment paper and place a wire rack on each sheet. Lightly brush each rack with oil.

Arrange the halved tomatoes on the racks, cut-side up, then sprinkle with the herbs, salt, and pepper.

Place one sheet on the top rack and the other on the bottom. Roast for 2 hours, then switch the two racks. Continue roasting until the tomatoes have shrunk by approximately half and are dry to the touch, about another 2 hours.

Remove from the oven, take the racks off of the baking sheets, and let cool completely. Use the oven-dried tomatoes immediately or transfer to 1-quart mason jars and cover with the olive oil. They will keep in the refrigerator for up to 2 weeks. (You can store unused oven-roasted tomatoes dry, as opposed to in oil, but I like the resulting product much less: Go with the oil.)

NOTE: Create a flavorful garnish akin to Scallion Salt (page 184) by freezing 1 cup Oven-Dried Tomatoes until brittle, then transfer the frozen tomatoes to a high-speed blender or food processor. Starting on low and increasing the speed to high, grind the tomatoes to a powder. Mix with 1 teaspoon salt, if desired—makes about ¼ cup.

This recipe employs the traditional method; however, if you've invested in sous-vide equipment, poaching eggs is another way to deploy that tool in your arsenal.

POACHED EGGS

MAKES 4

Salt
1 tablespoon distilled vinegar
4 large eggs

Bring 6 cups of salted water and the vinegar to a boil in a medium pot, then reduce the heat to maintain a simmer, about 200°F on an instant-read thermometer.

Carefully break an egg into a small bowl, then tip the egg into the water. Swirl the water gently with a wooden spoon for about 10 seconds, just until the egg begins to set. Repeat straining and tipping with the remaining eggs. Cook, swirling occasionally, until the egg whites are fully set but the yolks are still soft, about 4 minutes. Carefully lift the eggs from the pot using a slotted spoon. Serve immediately.

HERB
OIL

CHILE
OIL

This is a tremendously simple recipe—actually, more of a technique—that can be varied to create a nearly endless set of flavors that add beauty and elegance to numerous dishes. An herb-infused oil can be a delicious garnish for meat but absolutely shines simply drizzled into a rustic soup or on top of a sauce. That is how it's used in the Short Rib Goulash (page 87). It could be a wonderful garnish on, for example, the New York Strip Steak with Mushroom and Red Wine Reduction (page 143).

As with the Scallion Salt (page 184), there is no magic to the specific mix of soft, fresh herbs. Get used to making this recipe. It is incredibly useful, if for no other reason to help decrease food waste. We all have fresh herbs breaking down somewhere in our refrigerator.

Depending on whether your herb oil is intended primarily as a visual or finishing element, season the oil with salt as you would anything else going onto the plate. If you plan to cook with the oil, however, don't add salt.

HERB OIL

MAKES ABOUT 1 CUP

4 cups loosely packed tender green herbs, such as parsley, basil, chives, oregano, dill, or fennel fronds, or a mixture (leaves only, no stems—see Note)

1 cup grapeseed, canola, or another neutral oil

Bring a medium pot of water to a boil. As it is coming up to temperature, make an ice bath by putting ice in a large bowl or pot and adding 3 cups of water. When the water comes to a boil, add the herbs and boil just long enough to wilt, 20 to 30 seconds. Immediately remove and transfer to the ice bath. (The point of this step is to bring out and fix in place the bright green color of the fresh herbs; without blanching, once cut, the herbs would quickly blacken.)

Once cooled, drain the herbs well, wrap in a clean kitchen towel, and squeeze out as much of the water as possible—be gentle but thorough. Excess water will have a substantial effect on the final product.

Transfer the herbs and oil to the bowl of a high-speed blender or food processor. Blend, starting on low speed and moving to high, allowing the heat of the blender as well as its force to break down the herbs and turn the oil a brilliant green color, about 1 minute.

Line a fine-mesh strainer with cheesecloth with a large bowl beneath it. Pour the mixture from the blender through, allowing gravity to do the work—do not press on the solids. Give it some time, at least 15 to 20 minutes, to drain completely into the bowl. Store the herb oil in a sealed container in the refrigerator for up to a few months.

NOTE: While you can make any herb oil using the recipe above by simply altering which herb leaves you use, it is slightly different for cilantro. Why? Because the highest concentration of flavor in fresh cilantro is found in the stems. So, follow the recipe above but use whole sprigs of cilantro, including the tender stems, not just the leaves.

Like herb oils, Chile Oil can be either a finishing element or a cooking medium. You can easily manipulate the level of heat by changing the type of chile you're using to make the oil. Chiles de arbol, for example, are on the hotter end of the scale. Guajillo chiles are considerably milder but still offer that beautiful reddish-orange glow.

While it's tempting to focus on the visual aspects of chile oils, they can add a lot to a dish when used as a cooking oil. It's a technique used frequently in China. Cooking in a chile oil can add a spicy underlayer to any dish.

CHILE OIL

MAKES ABOUT 1 CUP

1 cup grapeseed, canola, or another neutral oil

3 whole dried red chiles (árbol chiles or guajillos for a milder flavor)

2 tablespoons red chile flakes

Heat 2 tablespoons of the oil in a small saucepan over medium heat. Add the whole chiles and cook, stirring, for 30 seconds, then stir in the red chile flakes and continue cooking until they start to sizzle, about another 30 seconds. Monitor the heat and do not let them get too brown. If they go too far, you will have to start over.

Add the remaining oil to the pot. Heat until warmed through, about 1 minute. Remove from the heat and let cool to room temperature. Transfer the mixture, including the solids, to an airtight bottle or jar. Shake the container occasionally to disperse the chiles. Keep in the refrigerator for up to 2 years. The oil will look cloudy when refrigerated; allow it to come back to room temperature before using and it will look clear again.

onfits are, traditionally, any type of food cooked slowly over a long period of time for the purpose of preservation. But they've long since gone past that original purpose and have become a method of intensifying flavor. Take, for example, this cherry tomato confit. The little red jewels suspended in olive oil burst with flavor and are keys to dishes like the Israeli Couscous with Asparagus and Tomato Confit (page 193) and the Risotto of Mushrooms and Peas with Tomato Confit (page 117). Slicing the garlic cloves both lends a richer, rounder flavor than minced garlic and leaves you with the delicious slices, which turn into soft, golden petals from their long bath in the olive oil.

TOMATO CONFIT

MAKES 3 CUPS

30 cherry tomatoes
4 cloves garlic, sliced
2 cups extra-virgin olive oil

Combine the cherry tomatoes, garlic, and oil in a small saucepan. Place over medium heat and bring to a boil. Immediately reduce the heat to maintain a simmer and cook until the tomatoes just start to split, about 30 minutes. Transfer to a glass quart jar and refrigerate. The tomato confit will keep in the refrigerator for up to 1 week.

NOTE: Use this same technique to make a confit from the flesh of red peppers left over from the Red Pepper Skin Curls (page 196).

The oil from this tomato confit can be a valuable ingredient in and of itself, as in the Veal Stew with Preserved Lemon, Olives, and Charred Tomato-Oil Scallions (page 135).

Take your time with this recipe. While it is certainly possible to hit fast forward by cooking on a higher temperature or by adding water to promote caramelization, the final product will suffer. Time and low temperature are your friends. Onion confit can be prepared using either butter or schmaltz. If you're using it with a meat dish, use schmaltz. It can be used with nearly any dish to add another layer of deeply satisfying, savory flavor.

ONION CONFIT

MAKES ABOUT 1½ CUPS

1 tablespoon butter or Schmaltz (page 187)

1 tablespoon extra-virgin olive oil

2 medium yellow onions, thinly sliced

½ teaspoon salt

1 tablespoon sugar

3 tablespoons white wine vinegar

Combine the butter (or schmaltz) and olive oil in a medium sauté pan over low heat. Add the onions and salt and cook, stirring occasionally, until softened and translucent, 15 to 20 minutes. If the onions begin to dry out, add water 1 tablespoon at a time (you're not looking for caramelization yet).

Stir in the sugar and vinegar and continue cooking over low heat, stirring occasionally, until onions are pasty and caramelized, another 15 minutes.

The onion confit will keep in the refrigerator for up to 1 week.

Classic gremolata is a dry fresh herb "sauce" of lemon, parsley, and garlic. It's a simple and perfectly balanced but zippy combination of ingredients that's perfect for Italian-inflected dishes. But use 1 bunch of cilantro, including tender stems, in place of the parsley and swap 2 limes in for the lemon and it works perfectly with Latin dishes.

In this book I use a gremolata with the Pan-Roasted Lamb Chops with Italian Salsa Verde (page 138), but it could just as well be a zesty addition to the New York Strip Steak with Mushroom and Red Wine Reduction (page 143) or any rich, savory dish that could benefit from a bright pop of freshness.

CLASSIC GREMOLATA

MAKES ABOUT ⅓ CUP

1 lemon

1 bunch fresh parsley, finely minced

1 clove garlic, finely minced

Salt and freshly ground black pepper

Using a zester, remove about 1 teaspoon of lemon zest. Keep in mind that the zest is the outer peel, not the inner white pith—be careful not to include any of the pith below the skin because it will be bitter. Combine the minced zest with the parsley and garlic in a bowl and season with salt and black pepper.

Store any unused gremolata in an airtight container in the refrigerator for up to 1 day.

Curls are a very easy way of adding both an attractive and flavorful garnish to any dish using just knife skills, a bell pepper, and water. If you want a bit more flavor, use distilled vinegar in place of the water. Try a different colored pepper for a more festive garnish—green, yellow, and orange bell peppers work fine, as do large chiles, such as poblanos or Anaheims.

You can change the flavor profile totally by using the same technique with scallion greens. Just cut the scallion tops open and slice them lengthwise very thinly, then run the back of your knife along the inside of each of the slices.

RED PEPPER SKIN CURLS

1 large red bell pepper

Using a vegetable peeler or paring knife, cut long and thin slices of peel off the bell pepper. Reserve the flesh of the pepper for another purpose, perhaps to make pepper confit using the same technique as the Tomato Confit (page 193) recipe. Cut the slices of skin into long strings as narrow as you can make them and drop each into a bowl of cold water. Using your hand, fluff up the strings in the water. You will see them begin to curl up. Allow them to soak for 5 minutes. They will have a tendency to clump together—simply separate them and they are ready for use immediately (which they should be as they don't store well).

Croutons are essential to many dishes in this book, including the Original Caesar's Restaurant Bar Caesar Salad (page 95), Spanish Garlic Soup with Oven-Dried Tomatoes and Sourdough Croutons (page 97), Gazpacho with Croutons (page 98), and California Fisherman's Cioppino (page 125). This recipe calls for butter but if you'd like to use these croutons with a meat dish, just use Schmaltz (page 187) instead.

CROUTONS

MAKES ABOUT 10 TO 15 CROUTONS (DEPENDING ON THE SIZE OF THE SLICES)

1 clove garlic, sliced

2 tablespoons extra-virgin olive oil

2 tablespoons butter

1 small French baguette

Lightly crush the garlic clove slices, put them in a ramekin or small bowl, cover with the olive oil, and infuse overnight.

Preheat the oven to 350°F.

Remove garlic slices from the oil. Melt the butter in a small skillet over low heat, then mix with garlic oil. Cut the baguette into thick slices and brush each with the garlic butter. Arrange on a cookie sheet or oven-safe tray. Bake for 3 to 4 minutes, until firm but not hard. If topping a Caesar salad, bake until crispy, another minute or so.

Store the croutons in an airtight container at room temperature for up to 3 days or in the freezer for up to 2 weeks.

RECIPE INDEX

INDEX

(Page references in *italics* refer to illustrations.)

V

veal:
    Piccata, 137
    Stew with Preserved Lemon, Olives, and Charred
        Tomato-Oil Scallions, *134*, 135–36
Vegetable Stock, *153*, 154
    Roasted, 155
Vietnamese "Jewish Penicillin" (Pho Ga with Matzo
        Noodles), 30–31

vinaigrettes:
    Asparagus, 60, *61*
    Dill, Fresh, 102, *103*
    Lemon and Red Wine, 175
Vitamix, 17

W

Whitefish, Smoked, Knishes, 70

ACKNOWLEDGEMENTS

The process of writing this book has been a lengthy one that stretches back through seasons of life. My partner in that life and in that process has always been my wife and love, Nancy Gardiner. And she has been more than "just" that. She has been my sounding board, recipe taster and tester, my sous chef and critic, and she has been my support system in more ways than I could say because some of them I have not yet sussed out.

My parents, Edwin and Wita Gardiner have been constant champions reminding me of what I'd promised myself and turning over the laboratory to me, pretending everything was delicious and gorgeous even when it wasn't, but in ways that gave me peek-a-boos of the truth. My daughter, Gwennie, ate more of the dishes of various iterations of this book than any child should be subjected to when all they really wanted was the stuff out of that blue box. It was my sister, Jacqueline's first marriage to Marc Feldman, an observant Jew, that was the spark leading to this book. She, her daughters (Anna and Natasha), Marc, and her current husband Mike have been continuing muses and experimental subjects that richly merit thanks.

I owe a huge debt of gratitude to David Rolland, my first editor at San Diego CityBeat, who taught me the difference between a self-indulgent blog and the standard for print. Subsequent editors— Seth Combs, Ron Donaho, and Christina Fuoco— have each continued that education in different ways as has Christine Ross at the *San Diego Union-Tribune*. I also owe thanks to Diane Benaroyo at *L'Chaim San Diego Magazine* for the opportunity to first bring my kosher recipes to a print audience.

Thank you to the many chefs who have given me the opportunity to come into their kitchens and stage, cook, learn, and come to understand the standard of professionalism: William Bradley, Chad White, Iker Castillo, Bo Bendana Sein, as well as William Eick, Amy DiBiase, Drew Bent, and Davin Waite. The latter, in particular, has been a constant source of inspiration. As he and his wife, Jessica, near the opening of their new vegan restaurant, they (along with Danielle Petke and Brian Rubin) helped point me in a crucial direction. I owe very special thanks to Ruth Henricks and Special Delivery for giving me the opportunity to "run" something and create in a professional kitchen setting.

Thank you to my incredible photography team. I doubt I'll ever see the quality and creativity of Sam Wells's photography surpassed. He made my good-looking dishes look better and made some I questioned look far better than I thought they could possibly ever look. Thanks to Euphemia Ng, Michelle Honig, and Daniel Bear for critical help in the kitchen, for the photography, and teaching Nancy and me things we did not know about ourselves. This book likely would not have happened without Jaime Fritsch's photography for the book proposal.

Thank yous are also in order for our food friends, Christina and Steve Wickman, Fred and Carla Sorilla, and Rob Colosia and Nicole Verdugo Preston, fellow denizens of the Jewish Cooking and San Diego Food Fanatic groups on Facebook, and my friends and broadcast partners—Jack Monaco, Sheen Fisher, and Mercy Baron—on the *Art of Spooning/All Forked Up* podcasts on the Specialty Produce Network. Indeed, thanks to Specialty Produce and Catalina Offshore Products (Tommy Gomes) for their amazing and inspiring ingredients.

This book likely would never have seen the light of day but for Deborah Ritchken, my agent, who saw something in the quirky idea of an upscale, uncompromising kosher cookbook and worked beyond the call of duty to make it happen. When it did, I initially thought it was confirmation I knew how to write a recipe. Jono Jarrett showed me I was wrong in his own enthusiastic, gentle, cajoling, and encouraging way. Perhaps now I really do know how to write a recipe thanks to him.

Lastly, I also owe thanks to Jack (as in "in the Box") for giving me my first job behind a stove and to the Oakland fire for making me want to cook a lot more.

MODERN KOSHER
Global Flavors, New Traditions

First published in the United States of America by
Rizzoli International Publications, Inc.
300 Park Avenue South
New York, NY 10010
www.rizzoliusa.com

Photographs © Sam Wells
www.samwellsphoto.com

Publisher: Charles Miers
Editor: Jono Jarrett
Design: Vertigo Design/Alison Lew
Production Manager: Colin Hough-Trapp
Managing Editor: Lynn Scrabis

Printed in China
2020 2021 2022 2023 / 10 9 8 7 6 5 4 3 2 1

ISBN: 978-0-8478-6875-9
Library of Congress Call Number: 2020935847

Visit us online:
Facebook.com/RizzoliNewYork
Twitter: @Rizzoli_Books
Instagram.com/RizzoliBooks
Pinterest.com/RizzoliBooks
Youtube.com/user/RizzoliNY
Issuu.com/Rizzoli